NEW TESTAMENT MESSAGE

A Biblical-Theological Commentary

Wilfrid Harrington, O.P. and Donald Senior, C.P.

EDITORS

New Testament Message, Volume 11

2 CORINTHIANS

Francis T. Fallon

VERITAS PUBLICATIONS / DUBLIN

Published by
VERITAS PUBLICATIONS
7-8 Lower Abbey Street, Dublin

in cooperation with

MICHAEL GLAZIER, INC.
Wilmington, Delaware 19801

Library of Congress Catalog Card Number: 80-80319
International Standard Book Number
    New Testament Message series: 0-89453-123-9
    2 Corinthians: 0-89453-134-4

This investigation was supported by University of Kansas General Research allocation 3037-20-0038 and
3234-20-0038.

Printed in the Republic of Ireland by Genprint Ltd.

Contents

Philipo amico meo.

EDITORS' PREFACE

New Testament Message is a commentary series designed to bring the best of biblical scholarship to a wide audience. Anyone who is sensitive to the mood of the church today is aware of a deep craving for the Word of God. This interest in reading and praying the scriptures is not confined to a religious elite. The desire to strengthen one's faith and to mature in prayer has brought Christians of all types and all ages to discover the beauty of the biblical message. Our age has also been heir to an avalanche of biblical scholarship. Recent archaeological finds, new manuscript evidence, and the increasing volume of specialized studies on the Bible have made possible a much more profound penetration of the biblical message. But the flood of information and its technical nature keeps much of this scholarship out of the hands of the Christian who is eager to learn but is not a specialist. *New Testament Message* is a response to this need.

The subtitle of the series is significant: "A Biblical-Theological Commentary." Each volume in the series, while drawing on up-to-date scholarship, concentrates on bringing to the fore in understandable terms the specific message of each biblical author. The essay-format (rather than a word-by-word commentary) helps the reader savor the beauty and power of the biblical message and, at the same time, understand the sensitive task of responsible biblical interpretation.

A distinctive feature of the series is the amount of space given to the "neglected" New Testament writings, such as Colossians, James, Jude, the Pastoral Letters, the Letters of Peter and John. These briefer biblical books make a significant but often overlooked contribution to the richness of the New Testament. By assigning larger than normal coverage to these books, the series hopes to give these parts of Scripture the attention they deserve.

Because *New Testament Message* is aimed at the entire English speaking world, it is a collaborative effort of international proportions. The twenty-two contributors represent biblical scholarship in North America, Britain, Ireland and Australia. Each of the contributors is a recognized expert in his or her field, has published widely, and has been chosen because of a proven ability to communicate at a popular level. And, while all of the contributors are Roman Catholic, their work is addressed to the Christian community as a whole. The New Testament is the patrimony of all Christians.It is the hope of all concerned with this series that it will bring a fuller appreciation of God's saving Word to his people.

Wilfrid Harrington, O.P.
Donald Senior, C.P.

INTRODUCTION

PAUL'S SECOND EPISTLE to the Corinthians is the most personal and also the most perplexing of his epistles. It is the most personal of his letters in that here he shows his own understanding of his apostolate, he attacks the opponents of his apostolate, and he engages in reconciliation with his Corinthian converts. At the same time this letter is also the most perplexing of his epistles in that it is fraught with historical, literary, and religious problems. Nevertheless, a careful reading of the letter and consideration of these problems can be richly rewarding. Thereby, the letter will reveal a person passionately committed to his faith and call as an apostle. It will also reveal the religious principles which undergirded a life of service as an apostle. Before we discuss the various problems associated with this letter, we shall turn first to the situation prior to the composition of 2 Corinthians.

On a missionary journey Paul had arrived at Corinth in the Roman province of Achaia probably late in the year 49 or early in 50. According to the report in the Acts of the Apostles (18:11), he stayed there for a year and a half. Then he was brought before the Roman pro-consul Gallio for interrogation—probably in the spring of 51. Shortly thereafter he left for Ephesus (Acts 18:18-19). The Acts of the Apostles then records a departure from Ephesus, a stay in Antioch, and then a return through Galatia to Ephesus where he spent about three years (Acts 18:20-23; 19:1-10; 20:31)—probably the period from the summer of 52 to spring of 55. It is also likely that toward the end of this period Paul suffered an imprisonment at Ephesus (cf. 2 Cor

1

1:8-10). During this lengthy stay in Ephesus it is evident that Paul also received news from Corinth and questions concerning the association of some Corinthians with immoral persons. Paul responded to these questions in an initial letter to the Corinthians, which is now lost to us (1 Cor 5:9-11). Later he sent Timothy to Corinth (1 Cor 16:10). Next Paul received a delegation and a letter from the Corinthian community. Then he answered their letter in the epistle that is preserved for us as 1 Corinthians. In this epistle he announced his plans to remain in Ephesus until Pentecost (probably in spring 54) and then travel through Macedonia to Corinth (1 Cor 16:5-6). Thus far the events prior to the writing of 2 Corinthians are clear. However, subsequent events are more problematic.

HISTORICAL PROBLEMS AND THEORIES

Concerning the following events the Acts of the Apostles is remarkably terse. It states simply as follows:

> "Now after these events Paul resolved in the Spirit to pass through Macedonia and Achaia and go to Jerusalem, saying, 'After I have been there, I must also see Rome.' And having sent into Macedonia two of his helpers, Timothy and Erastus, he himself stayed in Asia for a while" (19:21-22).

Next, the Acts of the Apostles reports on the disturbance caused by the pagan craftsmen against Paul (19:23-41) and then concludes its account of Paul's final journey and final visit to Corinth in these words:

> "After the uproar ceased, Paul sent for the disciples and having exhorted them took leave of them and departed for Macedonia. When he had gone through these parts and had given them much encouragement, he came to Greece. There he spent three months, and when a plot

was made against him by the Jews as he was about to set sail for Syria he determined to return through Macedonia" (20:1-3).

In order to obtain a more complete picture of the events during this period, one must draw upon 2 Corinthians. It is clear from 2 Cor 9:1-4 that Paul is writing from Macedonia during his final journey, but it is also clear from 2 Cor 12:14 and 13:1 that this final visit to Corinth will be a third visit. Thus there must have been another visit, which is not recorded by the Acts of the Apostles. It seems likely that this "intermediate" visit occurred after rather than before the writing of 1 Corinthians. Further, from chs. 10-13 it is evident that during this visit Paul was attacked by other missionary apostles and that he was not defended by the Corinthians. In addition, from 2 Cor 2:5-10 and 7:12 it is clear that Paul suffered some offense during his intermediate visit to Corinth. The nature of the offense and identity of the offender remain problems. However, it seems unlikely that this offender is to be identified with the incestuous person of 1 Cor 5:1-2, as some scholars previously theorized. Further in 2 Cor 2:3-4 and 7:8-9 Paul refers to a letter written with many tears. Scholars have questioned whether these verses refer to the initial lost letter, to 1 Corinthians, to another lost letter, or to a letter which is at least partially preserved in our canonical 2 Corinthians.

Further problems arise concerning the two companions of Paul—Timothy and Titus. As we noted earlier, 1 Cor 16:10 indicates that Timothy had been sent to Corinth. There is no report that he arrived in Corinth or that he returned to Ephesus. If, however, the hypothesis here followed is correct that the Philippian correspondence and the letter to Philemon were written from a prison in Ephesus towards the end of Paul's stay there, then Timothy must have returned to Ephesus since he is mentioned in the letter openings as well as Paul (Phil 1:1; cf. 1:7; Philemon 1). He is also with Paul then in Macedonia as 2 Cor 1:1 attests. Concerning Titus in 2 Corinthians, there are three different sets of references to his visits to Corinth. He is the bearer of the letter of tears (2 Cor 2:12-13; 7:5-16). He also is sent to arrange the collection (2 Cor 8:16-23) at a time in which Paul was at peace with the Corinthian community (2 Cor 8:8-11). Further, Titus is defended as not defrauding the Corinthians during his visit with them to arrange the collection (2 Cor 12:16-18). A problem arises if the references in chs. 8 and 12 are to the same visit; for in ch. 8 the visit is treated as imminent whereas in ch. 12 it is treated as past. It is more likely, however, that ch. 12 refers to one visit and ch. 8 to a later visit.

LITERARY PROBLEMS AND THEORIES.

In addition to these historical problems, 2 Corinthians also presents a number of literary problems. We shall discuss briefly then the difficulties, the main theories offered to meet these difficulties, and the hypothesis followed in this commentary.

As one reads 2 Corinthians there is an evident break in the train of thought from 2:13 to 2:14 and again from 7:4 to 7:5. In the verses up to 2:13 Paul has been discussing his travels to Troas and Macedonia as he awaited the arrival of Titus. Then in 2:14-7:4 there is a lengthy discussion and defense of his apostolate. Finally in 7:5-16 Paul's joy at the arrival of Titus in Macedonia and the news of the Corinthians' repentance and return to Paul are recounted. The discontinuity in thought is so great that a number of scholars have postulated not simply a digression by Paul but separate documents by Paul. Looked at in themselves, the chapters 2:14-7:4 appear to these scholars as part of a "Letter of Defense" by Paul of his apostolate. Chapters 1:1-2:13 and their conclusion in 7:5-16 then appear as a "Letter of Reconciliation" between Paul and his community. This letter would probably have been written at a later period after

Paul's defense of his apostolate had failed and a break with the community had occurred.

A similar problem is met within the "Letter of Defense" in the transition from 6:13 to 6:14 and from 7:1-2. In the verses preceding 6:13 Paul has addressed the Corinthians. He exhorts them to widen their hearts for him. In 6:14-7:1, however, the exhortation is not to be associated with unbelievers. Then in 7:2-4 the Corinthians are again exhorted to open their hearts to Paul. Here too commentators are led to suggest that more than a simple digression is involved; there are different documents. In addition, the passage 6:14-7:1 contains a number of words and thoughts either not found in or contrary to Paul's other writings. As a result a number of scholars consider this passage to be a fragment not written by Paul and later inserted or interpolated into this part of 2 Corinthians.

When one considers chs. 8 and 9, another problem emerges. Both chapters deal with the collection. However, first of all, the transition from ch. 7 to ch. 8 is difficult, since a different situation is presumed in each case. Both chapters are written from Macedonia (7:5; 8:2); but in 7:5 Paul writes in the midst of afflictions whereas in 8:1-2 the afflictions of the churches in Macedonia are past. It seems likely that the afflictions referred to are the same and thus that 7:5-16 was written at a different time than ch. 8. Further, ch. 9 discusses the same subject as ch. 8, the collection, without ever alluding to the previous discussion. It is also clearly addressed to the churches of Achaia (9:1-2). Thus again some scholars have suggested that ch. 9 was originally an independent letter.

Chapters 10-13 present the final literary problem. The sharp break in tone with the preceding chapters is manifest. Previously the spirit of the letter was one of reconciliation and appeal for the collection whereas these four chapters suddenly launch into an aggressive and sarcastic attack upon opponents and accusation against the community. Again, the break seems so sharp that some scholars have posited the separate existence of chs. 10-13.

These literary difficulties in 2 Corinthians have given rise to a number of theories. The unity of the epistle, the traditional view, is still maintained by some scholars, such as Dillon in the *Jerome Biblical Commentary*. The difficult transitions in the text are then explained as the result of pauses in dictation by Paul or as the result of the arrival of fresh information to Paul. Other scholars propose that our present 2 Corinthians is a collection of letters. A simpler form of this hypothesis has been advocated most recently by Barrett in the *Harper's New Testament Commentaries*. He suggests that chs. 1-9 were the original letter and that chs. 10-13 were written later and afterwards added to the letter. A more complex form of the theory was offered by Bornkamm (*The Unity and Integrity of the New Testament*) in which a series of letters between Paul and the Corinthians was later collected by an editor into our present 2 Corinthians.

The following hypothesis, which draws upon the theory of Bornkamm, will be utilized in this commentary. Probably in the spring of 54 Paul in Ephesus learned that other wandering christian missionaries had arrived in Corinth and that the Corinthians desired a visit from him soon. Shortly thereafter Paul wrote a "Letter of Defense" (2:14-6:13; 7:2-4) and sent it probably with Titus who was to counter the missionaries with it, to reestablish the authority of Paul, to hasten the collection and to announce Paul's change of plans, i.e. his intention to visit Corinth before his trip to Macedonia and then again on his return. Within a short time news arrived from Corinth, perhaps by the return of Titus, that the situation was still critical in Corinth. Then, probably in the summer of 54, Paul visited Corinth; he endured the offense of 2 Cor 2:5-6; he perceived the wavering, if not the withdrawal, of the Corinthians from his authority; and he returned dejectedly to Ephesus, perhaps through Macedonia and without returning to Corinth. Later, probably in the fall of 54, Paul sent a "Letter of Tears" (chs. 10-13) by Titus to the Corinthians in which he reasserted his apostolic right, attacked his opponents, and recalled the Corinthians to his gospel. Subsequently, in the winter of 54, he endured imprisonment in Ephesus (2 Cor 1:8-10). After his release, in the spring of 55, he left Ephesus to preach in Troas and to await the arrival of Titus. When Titus did not appear, he hastened on to Macedonia where he met Titus, received the good news of the return of the Corinthians to Paul's authority, and wrote to them a "Letter of Reconciliation" (1:1-2:13; 7:5-16). Probably slightly later, in the summer of 55, he wrote a "Letter of Reconciliation for Titus and the Brethren" (ch. 8) concerning the collection and sent them to Corinth with it. Then, probably in the fall of 55, he wrote another "Letter of Recommendation for the Brethren" (cf. 9) and sent them with it to arrange the collection in Achaia. Paul himself then traveled to Corinth and spent the winter of 55 there, where he wrote his Letter to the Romans before his trip to Jerusalem and then to Rome.

A final part of the hypothesis of Bornkamm, upon which we should like to draw, is that someone later collected and edited these letters into one epistle. He suggests that this occurred later in the century, that the person was probably a Corinthian, and that he considered it as a last testament of Paul. In Acts 20 we know that Luke presents Paul as delivering a last speech or testament. It is also clear that the common features of this genre include a reference to the point of death and to what God has done in one's past life, an exhortation to observe God's commands, a look into future trials and persecutions for the descendants, and a prayer for the descendants. One can see that an editor might plausibly have had this scheme in mind as he collected the letters of Paul and also added the fragment 6:14-7:1. There is the reference to a point of death (1:8-9) and to one's past life (1:10-2:17). The passage 6:1-7:4 could be construed as exhortation. Chs. 10-13 could be taken as the prediction of false apostles in the future, and the epistle closes with a prayer.

HISTORICAL RELIGIOUS PROBLEMS

A third set of problems concerning 2 Corinthians pertains to the History of Religions. It is necessary to have some understanding concerning the Corinthians and the opponents of Paul before one can appreciate fully the thought of Paul himself. From the internal evidence of 1 Corinthians and 2 Corinthians we can infer that the Corinthian Christians belong mostly to the poorer social classes (1 Cor 1:26-29). In the main, the community must have been composed of former Gentiles (1 Cor 1:22-24). However, they must have been Gentiles who had previously been close to Judaism and to the synagogue, if we are to presume that in a short time they were able to understand Paul's involved scriptural argument (e.g. 1 Cor 10 and 2 Cor 3). Further, there must have been former Jews among the Corinthian Christians (1 Cor 1:21-25; 9:19-23).

Although some scholars have suggested that the Corinthian Christians were gnostics, it seems more likely that they were religious enthusiasts. The presence of God's spirit was an important part of their religious life, and they looked for the manifestation of the spirit in themselves and in the missionaries they accepted—a manifestation in speech and sign and ecstatic activity. Further, they emphasized saving, revealed knowledge rather than simply rational knowledge. In this respect, they share some tendencies with the gnostics who also stressed saving, revealed knowledge and added to that a belief in the evilness of creation and the divineness of the individual.

The opposing missionaries have also been variously identified by scholars. They have been termed Judaizers, i.e. those from Jerusalem who wanted to establish the necessity of observing the Law by all Christians. Others have suggested that they were Christian gnostics. More recently Georgi, a student of Bornkamm, has suggested in his monograph *The Opponents of Paul in 2 Corinthians* the more plausible thesis that the missionaries were "divine men," that is, those who claimed possession of the divine spirit and the consequent ability to perform great signs and wonders. It is clear that these missionaries had a Jewish origin (11:22) and claimed such possession of the spirit (11:4-6). It is also clear that they attacked Paul as not being a true apostle, as an ineffective speaker, as a tyrant (10:8), and a coward. As proof that he was not a true apostle, the opponents showed that Paul did not accept the maintenance of an apostle (11:7-9; 12:14).

The linguistic and cultural tradition upon which these missionaries drew was indirectly the Greco-Roman tradition and more directly the Hellenized-Jewish tradition. In the New Testament era many cults had spread throughout the Mediterranean area. There also were wandering missionaries for these cults and wandering philosophers. For these wanderers and for their audiences miracles were an important attestation of the presence of religious power, i.e. the missionaries needed to appear as "divine men." Within the Greco-Roman period Judaism appeared as another cult with its origins in Palestine but its dispersion throughout the civilized world. As its missionaries strove to defend Judaism, to explain it to the Gentiles, and to convince the Gentiles of its truth, they adopted the common language (Greek) and interpreted their jewish heritage in accord with the hopes and aspirations of their era. Thus, Abraham, Moses, and other heroes of jewish tradition, were presented as "divine men." Finally, as such Hellenized Jews became members of the Christian movement, they brought with them their tradition and applied it now to Jesus so that he became the "divine man" par excellence. In accord with this "divine-man" Christology, these christianized Jews became delegates of Jesus, his apostles, "divine men" invested with his spirit. Such probably is the background of these opponents of Paul in 2 Corinthians.

Paul responded to the attack of these opponents with his own sharp critique. In 1 Corinthians Paul had opposed the emphasis by the Corinthians on their sharing in the spirit and on their participating already in the resurrection. He accomplished this by stressing the reality of the cross of

Christ and the futurity of the Christian's share in the resurrection. Similarly in 2 Corinthians Paul responds to the opponents' emphasis on power and on miracle by his stress on the weakness and suffering not only of Christ but also of his apostle. Further, Paul attacks these missionaries as false apostles and agents of Satan (11:12-15).

For his position Paul too draws upon a linguistic and cultural tradition. His starting point is the message or kerygma of the death and resurrection of Jesus as Lord. In addition, he draws upon the teaching of the early church concerning Christ. Further, he draws upon his heritage of Hellenized Judaism in order to interpret the significance of Jesus. From jewish apocalyptic thought he stresses the future coming of Jesus. From jewish sapiential thought he speaks of the pre-existence of Christ. From the theme of the suffering wise or righteous person he interprets his own sufferings and those of his Lord. Finally, to refute his opponents Paul draws upon some of the polemical styles and usages popular in the Hellenistic world.

Although this letter has been written for a specific occasion, it has enduring value. It provides an inspiring example of a person committted to his community. Further, it shows a person concerned more about the well-being of his community than about his own aggrandizement.

In addition, this letter shows Paul's understanding of Christ, its implications for his life, and implicitly his challenge to his readers. For him christian apostolate and, by extension, christian existence cannot be a demonstration of power but rather must be a performance of service. The sufferings of Christ are to be paralleled by the daily service of the apostle and thus of the Christian to the community. Further, for Paul the life of the apostle and the Christian is not a life of self-satisfaction in the possession of spiritual experiences but a life marked by faith and service in the hope of future glory.

I. RECONCILIATION WITH THE COMMUNITY 2 COR 1:1 – 2:13.

THE BEGINNING.
2 Cor 1:1-2.

> **1** Paul, an apostle of Christ Jesus by the will of God, and Timothy our brother.
>
> To the church of God which is at Corinth, with all the saints who are in the whole of Achaia:
>
> ²Grace to you and peace from God our Father and the Lord Jesus Christ.

Second Corinthians begins with the opening of Paul's "Letter of Reconciliation" to the Corinthians. As usual in his letters Paul adopts the customary opening formula of a Greek letter and then modifies it and expands it with christian content. Typically a Greek letter opened simply with the name of the person sending the letter, then the name of the person to whom it was sent, and finally the term "greetings." Paul identifies himself not only by name but also by function as an apostle of Christ Jesus, that is, he is one "sent" by Christ Jesus. His task is to preach the gospel, and as such he possesses the authority of the one sending him. The basis for his mission is that he has seen the risen Lord (1 Cor 9:1; 15:3-8). Paul does not always identify himself as an apostle in his letters (cf. 1 Thess 1:1), but he does so when the issue of his apostolate has been raised (cf. Gal 1:1; 1 Cor 1:1). Thereby in the opening words there

is already a hint at the subject which receives a more extensive treatment in chs. 3-6 and 10-13. As an apostle Paul
considers himself to be such not by his own choice nor by
the commission of persons but rather by the mission of
Christ Jesus and ultimately by the decision of God.

In sending this letter Paul is not alone. He mentions his
co-worker Timothy, who is also listed in the addresses of
1 Thessalonians, Philippians, and Philemon (cf. also 2
Thessalonians and Colossians). In 1 Cor 4:17 Paul stated
that he had sent Timothy to Corinth and exhorted the
Corinthians to receive him when he arrived (16:10). However, from 2 Corinthians we gain no further information on
this visit of Timothy to Corinth. Presumably he reached
Corinth, then returned to Paul at Ephesus, and later traveled
into Macedonia from which this letter is being written
(2 Cor 2:12-13; 7:5-7; cf. Acts 19:21-22). Paul identifies
Timothy simply as a brother, that is, a brother Christian
but not an apostle.

As the recipients of the letter Paul designated first "the
church of God which is in Corinth." In using this terminology Paul draws upon the OT idea of Israel as the people
chosen by God and thus considers the Christians as the new
people of God. He refers then first of all to the church as a
whole before he specifies it as the church which is resident
in Corinth. In addition, the letter is designated for the other
christian communities in the province of Achaia, i.e. Greece.
This further designation of recipients may well come from
the final editor of the letters, who wished to give the composite letter a wider appeal. Again Paul assumes the
language of the OT in referring to the Christians as 'saints,"
i.e. those who have been made holy by the call of God rather
than by their own efforts.

Instead of the simple Greek term for greetings (*chairein*)
Paul draws upon the liturgical language of early Christianity
and wishes his recipients "grace" (*charis*) and "peace." By
"grace" he refers to the act of God in history, which is the
basis of christian existence. By "peace" he alludes to the
traditional jewish form of greeting *shalōm* and understands

by it the total state of well-being which results from God's redemptive act. His wish then for his Corinthian community is that they may apprehend more completely the grace and peace which they already enjoy. These are gifts from God, acknowledged as Father, and from Jesus Christ, proclaimed as Lord. In the Septuagint (the Greek translation of the OT; abbreviated hereafter as the LXX) the term "Lord" was applied to God whereas in the early church the title was used for Jesus in his eschatological role. For Paul the term refers to the present rule of Jesus and the obedience due him.

BLESSING FOR DELIVERANCE.
2 Cor 1:3-7.

> ³Blessed be the God and Father of our Lord Jesus Christ, the Father of mercies and God of all comfort, ⁴who comforts us in all our affliction, so that we may be able to comfort those who are in any affliction, with the comfort with which we ourselves are comforted by God. ⁵For as we share abundantly in Christ's sufferings, so through Christ we share abundantly in comfort too. ⁶If we are afflicted, it is for your comfort and salvation; and if we are comforted, it is for your comfort, which you experience when you patiently endure the same sufferings that we suffer. ⁷Our hope for you is unshaken; for we know that as you share in our sufferings, you will also share in our comfort.

In Greek letters the opening formula is very often followed by a thanksgiving. Normally Paul too begins his letters with a thanksgiving to God for the benefits received by his communities (cf. 1 Thess 1:2; 1 Cor 1:4). In so doing, Paul adopts the Greek custom but also adapts it in accord with Christian liturgical language and uses it to introduce the main themes of his letter. Here in 2 Corinthians Paul replaces the thanksgiving by a blessing, an alternate form of liturgical language probably because the blessing of God was more appropriate for comfort received in distress by

Paul himself as well as others. In identifying God as the Father of mercies and the God of comfort, Paul draws upon the language of the OT. Especially in Isaiah (40:1; 51:3, 12,19) God's saving act for his people is identified as "comforting."

The nature of the comforting offered to Paul is made clear in vs. 5. It is "through Christ," i.e. God's saving act in the sending of Christ as the eschatological event. Although the term "comfort" in its biblical sense can mean either to console or to deliver, it seems best to take it in the sense of "console" in order to have a consistent meaning throughout the pasage. Paul is consoled by the message of the gospel in all the tribulation that he experiences as an apostle in proclaiming the gospel. It is with this same consolation, i.e. the message of the gospel, that Paul can then console his Corinthian community. For Paul the life of an apostle is marked by sharing in the sufferings of Christ, i.e. experiencing sufferings as Christ did. But the apostle also shares in the redemption accomplished through Christ by his death and resurrection. If Paul suffers affliction then, he does so as an apostle in order that the Corinthians may accept the gospel and share in salvation. If on the other hand Paul receives consolation in the gospel, it is so that the Corinthians too might receive the gospel. At this point, Paul's thought takes an important turn. The Corinthians will be comforted or receive the gospel insofar as they endure the same sufferings which he endures. For Paul, just as the life of Christ was marked by suffering, so too the life of an apostle and of every Christian must be marked by suffering if it is to be authentically christian. In this view Paul suggests the main theme of the later chapters. The issue at hand will be the mode of life, which is a sign of the true apostle and the true Christian.

Paul concludes this section with a statement of confidence in the faith of the Corinthians. They share in the sufferings, i.e. by the encroachment of false apostles into their community, and thus show the signs of true christian existence. Therefore, Paul knows that they share in the gospel. Certainly in this blessing, then, Paul presents the main themes of his position but also sets a tone of acceptance of and reconciliation with his Corinthian Christians.

AN APOSTLE SUFFERS.
2 Cor 1:8-11.

> [8]For we do not want you to be ignorant, brethren, of the affliction we experienced in Asia; for we were so utterly, unbearably crushed that we despaired of life itself. [9]Why, we felt that we had received the sentence of death; but that was to make us rely not on ourselves but on God who raises the dead; [10]he delivered us from so deadly a peril, and he will deliver us; on him we have set our hope that he will deliver us again.
>
> [11]You also must help us by prayer, so that many will give thanks on our behalf for the blessing granted us in answer to many prayers.

Paul turns now from the opening and the blessing to the body of his letter by means of a formula of "disclosure," a phrase stating the author's desire that his addressee "know" something. Such a formula was often used in Greek letters and is also used elsewhere by Paul (cf. Rom 1:13). Immediately he discusses the main issue at hand, the sign that he is a true apostle—a mode of life marked by suffering. By means of the catchword "affliction" he links this paragraph with that of the blessing and introduces a specific instance of tribulation, an incident that befell him in the province of Asia.

Since Paul speaks in general terms about this incident, various theories have been proposed concerning the nature of the incident. Some scholars have suggested the riot in Ephesus against Paul recorded in Acts 19:23-40, while others have suggested a severe illness. More probable is the theory that Paul suffered imprisonment in Ephesus and that he feared for his life. In this experience of being sentenced to prison Paul sees the proper mode of existence of an apostle. He writes: "Why we feel that we have received the sentence of death; but that is to make us rely not on ourselves but on God who raises the dead." This translation is preferable to the RSV since the Greek uses the perfect tense, which expresses a past action that has a present effect. For Paul the true apostle is to be a suffering, righteous person. Just as righteous persons such as Joseph, Daniel, and Susanna were condemned but nevertheless delivered by God because of their trust in him, so too Paul bore the sentence of condemnation and continues to bear it while he trusts that God who delivered him before will deliver him again. Like those other righteous persons, the Maccabean martyrs, who were condemned but who also suffered death (cf. 2 Mac 7), Paul places his trust in the God who raises the dead for his ultimate rescue from death (cf. also the righteous, wise person who is condemned to death and later exalted by God in Wis 2:12-20 and 5:1-16).

In the meantime, he hopes for further deliverance from the sentence of death in order that he might continue his apostolic labors. He enlists the Corinthians' intercession with God on his behalf in this regard and joins their prayers with his own prayers and his own sufferings considered as a prayer for deliverance (cf. the sufferings of the Maccabean martyrs as a prayer in 2 Mac 7:37-38). By his further apostolic labors and their participation by prayer, Paul intends that greater thanks will be given to God for him by the many Christians. In typical Pauline fashion, however, the thanks given to God is not for Paul's own accomplishments but for the grace or blessing that has been given him, the grace to be an apostle and to preach the gospel message.

AN APOSTLE BOASTS ONLY IN THE GRACE OF GOD.
2 Cor 1:12-14.

> 12For our boast is this, the testimony of our conscience that we have behaved in the world, and still more toward you, with holiness and godly sincerity, not by earthly wisdom but by the grace of God. 13For we write you

nothing but what you can read and understand; I hope you will understand fully, [14]as you have understood in part, that you can be proud of us as we can be of you, on the day of the Lord Jesus.

As Paul continues his reconciliation with the Corinthians, he recalls one of the controversial terms, "boasting," and one of the charges against him, duplicity. In contrast to the opposing apostles who had entered Corinth and boasted in their own achievements (cf. 2 Cor 10:15-17; 11:10,16,18, etc.), Paul will boast only in the Lord. It is the theme of the apostle as a suffering, righteous person, which binds these two paragraphs. In the preceding paragraph Paul has depicted his sufferings. In this paragraph he presents himself as righteous—righteous by the gift of God. Just as the pure of heart (Ps 31:11), Wisdom (Sir 24:1,2), and the wise or righteous person (Sir 39:8; 1:11; 9:14-16) may boast, so too Paul boasts. But this acceptable type of boasting is boasting in the gift of God. Paul then boasts that as he considers himself in contrast to the way in which his opponents had considered him, he has conducted himself in the world in the holiness and sincerity which comes from God. He has not acted in accord with worldly wisdom but in accord with the true wisdom, which is a gift of God (cf. Wis 8:20-21 for wisdom as a gift of God to the wise person).

Paul then turns more directly towards the Corinthians and adds that especially toward them he has so conducted himself. He then takes up two elements of past misunderstanding to illustrate his correct action as an apostle to them. First, he asserts that he has not written letters with double meanings but only those which can be read and clearly understood. He will return to this issue in vss. 15-22. Secondly, the ground for his boasting shows him to be a true apostle. Paul's opponents had boasted of their success in making converts (10:8). Paul, however, would boast only of the power that had been given him for building up the church (7:14) and states that the day of the Lord, i.e. the final judgment, will show the ground for his boasting in the presence of the Corinthians who will be there as Christians. He further adds that as the Corinthians recognize this partial truth, he hopes that they will recognize the full truth in that he is the ground of their boasting, he is the apostle who proclaimed to them the gospel which they have accepted.

AS AN APOSTLE, PAUL IS TRUSTWORTHY; HIS TRAVEL PLANS.
2 Cor 1:15-22.

[15]Because I was sure of this, I wanted to come to you first, so that you might have a double pleasure; [16]I wanted to visit you on my way to Macedonia, and to come back to you from Macedonia and have you send me on my way to Judea. [17]Was I vacillating when I wanted to do this? Do I make my plans like a worldly man, ready to say Yes and No at once? [18]As surely as God is faithful, our word to you has not been Yes and No. [19]For the Son of God, Jesus Christ, whom we preached among you, Silvanus and Timothy and I, was not Yes and No; but in him it is always Yes.

[20]For all the promises of God find their Yes in him. That is why we utter the Amen through him, to the glory of God. [21]But it is God who establishes us with you in Christ, and has commissioned us; [22]he has put his seal upon us and given us his Spirit in our hearts as a guarantee.

Paul turns now to a specific issue in his writings that had evidently led some Corinthians to question his trustworthiness: his change in travel plans. He had originally decided to travel from Ephesus to Macedonia and then to Corinth before leaving for Jerusalem (1 Cor 16:5-8). We can infer from this passage that Paul had changed his plans so that he would travel from Ephesus first to Corinth, then to Macedonia, then again to Corinth, and finally on to Judea. It is clear—again from this passage—that after his trip from Ephesus to Corinth Paul failed to return to Corinth. Paul's aim is to defend the trustworthiness of his word as an apostle and then to admit that he did in fact change his plans (1:23-2:1). He explains the discrepancy as not deceit but as a change of mind, prompted by concern for the Corinthians.

Confident at that time of his correct relations with the Corinthians (vss. 12-14) Paul wanted to come to the Corinthians first. Later on his return trip he would visit them again so that they might have a second favor. He then asks ironically whether such plans for two visits could have been made out of fickleness or according to the flesh, i.e. in a way contrary to God (cf. Rom 8:4-5; Gal 5:16-17); he questions whether such plans could be construed as saying "yes" or "no" at the same time. Next in an oath formula Paul calls upon God to witness that his message is not "yes" and "no" at the same time. At this point, as Paul introduces the term "message," he launches into a theological digression, which is not entirely inappropriate since he wants to show a consistency between the gospel message he bears and the conduct of his own life. Concerning the gospel message Paul then adds that God's definitive "yes" has been spoken in Christ Jesus, the Son of God. This "yes" continues and is made present in the preaching of the gospel, which Paul, Silvanus, and Timothy have accomplished among the Corinthians. Paul adds that it is a "yes" or a fulfillment of all the promises made by God, i.e. the messianic promises of the OT. He then turns to the appropriate human response to this event, which is the liturgical expression "Amen" and which joins in the praise of God for the event of Jesus Christ. Just as God's act was through Jesus Christ, so for Paul praise of God in worship only occurs through Christ as well.

Paul continues his defense of his trustworthiness by referring to the continuing activity of God in the life of the Christian and by alluding to the initiation of that life in baptism. God has established Paul, his fellow-missionaries, and the Corinthians, as Christians and continues to maintain them in Christ (cf. 1 Cor 1:6,8). Thus Paul can assert his trustworthiness. The past event by which God brought one into Christ was baptism. Thus Paul draws upon the language of the baptismal tradition in the early church: anointing, sealing, and giving the Spirit. The anointing may refer to anointing with the Spirit (Acts 10:38) or to an actual anointing with oil as part of the baptismal ceremony. The sealing refers to baptism as a sign by which the baptized person is marked as belonging to God's people. The giving of the Spirit is associated with baptism and is considered here as the guarantee or, better, the first installment of the messianic blessings (cf. Eph 1:13-14; 4:30). Just as God is trustworthy, Paul wants to assert, so too is the person who has been called into christian existence and is maintained there by God.

PAUL'S APOSTOLIC PURPOSE
HAS BEEN MAINTAINED.
2 Cor 1:23-2:13.

[23]But I call God to witness against me—it was to spare you that I refrained from coming to Corinth. [24]Not that we lord it over your faith; we work with you for your joy, for you stand firm in your faith.
2 For I made up my mind not to make you another painful visit. [2]For if I cause you pain, who is there to make me glad but the one whom I have pained? [3]And I wrote as I did, so that when I came I might not be pained by those who should have made me rejoice, for I felt sure of all of you, that my joy would be the joy of you all. [4]For I wrote you out of much affliction and anguish of heart and with many tears, not to cause you pain but to let you know the abundant love that I have for you.
[5]But if any one has caused pain, he has caused it not to me, but in some measure—not to put it too severely— to you all. [6]For such a one this punishment by the majority is enough; [7]so you should rather turn to forgive and comfort him, or he may be overwhelmed by excessive sorrow. [8]So I beg you to reaffirm your love for him. [9]For this is why I wrote, that I might test you and know

whether you are obedient in everything. [10]Any one whom you forgive, I also forgive. What I have forgiven, if I have forgiven anything, has been for your sake in the presence of Christ, [11]to keep Satan from gaining the advantage over us; for we are not ignorant of his designs.

[12]When I came to Troas to preach the gospel of Christ, a door was opened for me in the Lord; [13]but my mind could not rest because I did not find my brother Titus there. So I took leave of them and went on to Macedonia.

As Paul continues in his "Letter of Reconciliation," he returns to the question of why he changed his plans and did not return to Corinth and then turns to the other lingering questions: why did he write such a severe letter and what should the community do about the offenders? As Paul answers these questions, he delicately alludes to the major issues of the past conflict. Equally delicately he evidences again his own position on these issues and indicates his own apostolic authority. These main issues are presented more completely in the major fragment of the severe letter or "Letter of Tears," which is preserved in chs. 10-13. Thus the delicate hints and allusions in 1:23-2:13 become clearer, when one traces these hints to their fuller statement in the later chapters.

Concerning his change in plans, Paul calls upon God as his witness that he changed his mind to spare the Corinthians. He had already warned them that if he came again with the conflict still unresolved, he would not spare them (13:2). Paul hastens to add that he writes this not as if he were lord over their faith. Thereby, he recalls the charge by his opponents that he was bold in his claim to authority, especially in his letters (10:1,8,10). Rather, as an apostle Paul claims to be a co-worker of their joy; he has proclaimed the gospel to them and they have accepted it, which is their source of joy. Further, now that the conflict is resolved and the Corinthians have returned to the gospel preached by Paul, Paul can be satisfied that after all they have not really accepted another gospel (11:4).

Paul then adds that he decided not to come again in sorrow. There is a seeming contradiction running through this passage in that Paul writes a letter in tears and in anguish of heart but never admits that he has been caused sorrow, although he does admit that he himself has caused sorrow. To understand this apparent contradiction it is important to realize that for Paul joy and sorrow do not refer just to the presence of conflict or friendship. Rather both terms can also have a reference to the gospel. Joy comes from sharing in the blessings of the messianic era through acceptance of the gospel (1:24, cf. Rom 14:17; Phil 3:1, 4:4-5); the apostle has a further joy as persons accept the gospel when he proclaims it. Sorrow, on the other hand, comes from rejection of the gospel (7:10), but there is also a "godly grief" that leads to repentance and acceptance of the gospel (7:10).

The sorrow which Paul caused the Corinthians on this "intermediate" visit seems to be the sorrow that arose from the conflict between Paul and the intruding apostles on the one hand and then Paul and the Corinthians on the other hand. Paradoxically the very ones who should cause Paul to rejoice, as he sees their progress in the gospel preached to them by him, are also the very ones who are saddened by Paul. Therefore, Paul asserts, he wrote this letter (chs. 10-13; cf. 13:10). He wrote this letter in anguish and in the midst of many tears not to sadden the Corinthians but to show them his love.

Paul now turns to the issue of the offenders. In contrast to the definite warning to the offenders in the community in 13:1-3, Paul now delicately raises as an hypothesis the possibility that there might have been an offender or offenders. Although this passage has often been interpreted to mean that there was a single person who caused a great offense to Paul during his intermediate visit, it is more probable that Paul is referring to those members of the Corinthian community who aligned themselves with the false apostles. As part of his effort at reconciliation, Paul is deliberately using indefinite language to refer to the offenders ("any one," "such a one") and thereby softening his remarks. In fact, Paul states, no offender has really caused him sorrow in the sense of turning him away from the gospel but rather has caused the community sorrow by attempting to persuade it to follow the false gospel of the opponents. In contrast to his warning about coming in severity (13:10), Paul adds here the qualifying and mollifying phrases that the sorrow has been caused "in some measure" and "not to put it too severely" to the Corinthians. Then Paul adds that the reproof to these offenders by the majority of the Corinthians who had remained faithful to Paul's gospel was now sufficient. The exact nature of the reproof is not clear; perhaps it was exclusion from the community. Paul exhorts the Corinthians to forgive such a person (or persons) and comfort him/them, probably in the sense of admitting him/them again to the community of those who share in the true gospel (cf. 1:4-5). Paul's fear is that otherwise he/they will be lost to Satan (2:11; cf. 10:12-15). For it is Satan who "overwhelms" or, better, "devours" (cf. 1 Pet 5:8); and there is a sorrow, a loss of share in the true gospel, that leads to death (cf. 2 Cor 7:10).

Paul then adds that the purpose of his letter was to determine their testing; whether they stood in the faith of the true gospel (cf. 13:5-8) and whether they were obedient to him as the apostle of the gospel (cf. 10:6). Thereby he glosses over his past attack on the opponents and his threat to punish every disobedience when the community restores its obedience to him (13:6). Since the Corinthians were the injured party, whomever they forgive Paul also forgives. Again Paul modifies his statement. Since he was not the injured party, he need not forgive but adds that insofar as he has forgiven, it is before Christ. The forgiveness consists in the restoration of the person/persons to the Christian community by the Corinthians; thereby the person/persons is/are freed from the threatening grasp of Satan. Paul refers here to Satan since he is convinced that his apostolate engages him in a contest with Satan (cf. 10:12-15).

II. PAUL'S DEFENSE OF
HIS APOSTOLATE
2 COR 2:14 – 6:13 and 7:2-4.

The abrupt change from Paul's report of his travels (2:13) to a thanksgiving to God (2:14) and then a lengthy defense of his apostolate (2:14-6:13; 7:2-4) signals a different source, another letter of Paul. In accord with the literary analysis offered in the introduction, this letter is termed his "Letter of Defense." It was probably written prior to his "intermediate" visit to Corinth. Evidently Paul had received a report that other Christian missionaries had entered Corinth. From the letter itself we can infer that Paul had an accurate insight into the theology of these missionaries and into the nature of their attack upon his own apostolate. Although Paul rebuts the attack of these opposing missionaries (cf. 3:1-3) and exposes his position clearly, the tone of anguish and fear of loss of the Corinthian Christians that is present in chs. 10-13 is missing in these chapters. Thus it seems that Paul still had high hopes of recalling the Corinthians to obedience at this point.

It would appear that a major fragment of the letter, although not the entire letter in which Paul defended his apostolate, has been preserved for us in 2 Corinthians. If the hypothesis be accepted that a later editor has collected these fragmentary letters and put them together with the model of a testament in mind, then one can understand why this "Letter of Defense" has been placed in just this position by the editor. A testament frequently begins with a narrative

of God's action in one's past life. Thus for the editor the
story of Paul's past apostolate as the divinely led, triumphant spread of the gospel would be stated near the
beginning of Paul's testament.

GOD'S SUPPORT OF HIS APOSTOLATE.
2 Cor 2:14-17.

> [14]But thanks be to God, who in Christ always leads us
> in triumph, and through us spreads the fragrance of the
> knowledge of him everywhere. [15]For we are the aroma of
> Christ to God among those who are being saved and
> among those who are perishing, [16]to one a fragrance from
> death to death, to the other a fragrance from life to life.
> Who is sufficient for these things? [17]For we are not, like
> so many, peddlers of God's word; but as men of sincerity,
> as commissioned by God, in the sight of God we speak
> in Christ.

Paul frequently opens his letters with a greeting and
then with a thanksgiving (e.g. 1 Cor 1:4-9). Thus this
thanksgiving in vs. 14 is probably taken from the opening
of Paul's "Letter of Defense." Further, the opening thanksgiving sentence in a Pauline letter usually hints at the main
themes to be developed in the letter. We shall see that this
fact helps to explain the packed formulation of Paul's
thought in vss. 14-17. Lastly, Paul's opening thanksgiving
usually gives thanks to God for blessings which the community has received and begins "I give thanks to God."
The slightly different formulation "To God (be) thanks"
may derive from the polemical situation in which Paul wants
to emphasize God and the ministry which he has received
rather than the blessings of the Corinthians.

As Paul thanks God for leading him in triumph, the very
word suggests that the emphasis is upon God (14). Further,
the term which Paul uses for a "triumph" is the term which

refers to the triumphal entry of the victorious general returning from war into his own capital and leading his soldiers and captives. It seems likely that Paul uses the term here to refer to himself as a captive, a slave of God in Christ. In contrast to the opposing missionaries in Corinth, who stress their possession of the spirit and their own power to evangelize successfully, Paul begins the defense of his own apostolate by placing his reliance upon God and by emphasizing that he is but a slave of God as a result of His saving act in Christ. Paul then draws upon the Jewish wisdom tradition to express his understanding of his apostolate. Like a messenger sent by Wisdom, Paul is sent by Christ and ultimately by God to spread the fragrance, which is the knowledge of God (15). The OT expression for a sacrifice as "a pleasing odor" (cf. Gen 8:21) had been reinterpreted in the Jewish wisdom tradition, and the two terms had been applied to wisdom as a fragrance (cf. Sir 24:15) and an aroma (cf. Wis 24:15). Paul then understands the gospel message which he preaches in the light of this tradition as the fragrance which spreads the knowledge of God.

Further, he understands himself as the "aroma of Christ" in the sense that not only his message but also his life witness to the wisdom which God has revealed in Christ, i.e. a wisdom in Christ's death and resurrection. Thus his preaching and his life manifest the event which inaugurated the new aeon in the world, the death and resurrection of Christ. Paul adds another thought in that he is the aroma of Christ for those who are in the process of being saved and for those who are in the process of perishing (16). The cryptic phrases which state that he is "to one a fragrance from death to death" and "to the other a fragrance from life to life" are best explained by reference to the remainder of the "Letter of Defense" (cf. especially 4:11-15) and seem to be hints of what is to come. The death of Christ is shown in the death or suffering which Paul as an apostle endures. Those who cannot find the gospel in the death of Christ or in the death of his apostle reject the gospel and enter into the death, by which they perish. The life of Christ is shown in the life of an apostle paradoxically when he is handed over to suffering or death (4:11). It is a life no longer lived for self but for God (5:15). Those who find the gospel in the life of Christ and in the paradoxical death and life of an apostle accept the gospel and enter into the life, by which they are being saved.

In typical Pauline fashion, Paul next takes over a key term and claim of the opponents, to be "sufficient" unto themselves, and implicitly denies their claim with the unanswered question as to who is sufficient to live the life of an apostle and to preach as an apostle. Like Moses in Ex 4:10 (LXX), Paul knows that he is not sufficient of himself but will affirm—in critical response to his opponents—that it is God who makes him sufficient (cf. 3:4-6). In a more directly polemical sentence, Paul accuses his opponents of "peddling God's word," of adulterating it and of selling it for pay (17). For his own part Paul recognizes that his preaching is based upon God's gift of sincerity and God's commission and that he carries on this task as a Christian in the presence of God.

THE COMMUNITY AS PAUL'S LETTER OF RECOMMENDATION.
2 Cor 3:1-3.

> 3 Are we beginning to commend ourselves again? Or do we need, as some do, letters of recommendation to you, or from you? ²You yourselves are our letter of recommendation, written on your hearts, to be known and read by all men; ³and you show that you are a letter from Christ delivered by us, written not with ink but with the Spirit of the living God, not on tablets of stone but on tablets of human hearts.

Paul begins his defense of his apostolate here. There are two points at issue. First, Paul is accused of recommending himself, and second, he is accused of lacking letters of recommendation. Letters to introduce and recommend

persons from one person or community to another were
customary in the ancient world. It seems that a specific type
of letter is in question here; i.e. a letter to attest that the bearers
were apostles and had evidenced the signs of the Spirit
within them (cf. 10:12,18; 12:1-3). With an ironical question
Paul rebuts the first charge (cf. 4:2; 5:12; 6:4). He responds
to the second charge by questioning whether he needs such
letters of recommendation (1). Then he uses a striking
metaphor: the community is his letter of recommendation
(2). As the bearer of the letter, Paul carries it with him;
however, the letter is not written on papyrus as was the
custom but was written in his heart. The use of the metaphor
is not completely consistent when Paul then adds that this
letter which is written in his heart, is known and read by
all men. It is intended in the sense that their existence as a
Christian community through the preaching of Paul is
sufficient demonstration of the authenticity of his apostolate and the presence of the Spirit. As Christians they
are visible to all and thus Paul's letter of recommendation.

In commenting upon the nature of the letter, Paul expands the metaphor in several ways with his opponents in
mind (3). First, he points out that Christ is the author of
the letter and thus that it is a heavenly letter. Further, it is
a letter delivered by him. Then Paul develops the idea of the
letter being "written in his heart" by a cluster of motifs.
He alludes to the Law of Moses that was written on stone
tablets by the finger of God (Ex 31:18), to the promise in
Jeremiah that God would form a new covenant and would
write his laws upon the hearts of his people (Jer 31:33), and
to the promise in Ezekiel that God would give a new spirit
to his people and would change their stony hearts into
fleshly hearts (Ezek 11:19; 36:26). Contrary to the Old
Testament Paul identifies the Law of Moses, the tablets of
stone, and the hearts of stone; he contrasts these with the
present work of God's Spirit. Evidently Paul expands his
reference to letters of recommendation by an allusion to
the Law of Moses because his opponents in their letters of

recommendation claim Moses and/or the Law for themselves. For Paul this is a claim merely to that which is external and not to that which is in the heart (cf. 5:12).

APOSTOLATE, NEW COVENANT, AND THE SPIRIT.
2 Cor 3:4-6.

> [4]Such is the confidence that we have through Christ toward God. [5]Not that we are sufficient of ourselves to claim anything as coming from us; our sufficiency is from God, [6]who has qualified us to be ministers of a new covenant, not in a written code but in the Spirit; for the written code kills, but the Spirit gives life.

In this passage Paul continues his defense of his apostolate by rooting it in God's commission within the new covenant. He expresses his confidence that the Corinthians are his letter of recommendation through Christ's agency (4). Again he returns to the theme of "sufficiency" (5), which was introduced in 2:16. Here Paul treats the theme more fully. Contrary to his opponents who consider themselves able to assess themselves and others and to claim certain powers as their own (cf. 2 Cor 10:2,7,11; 11:5; 12:6), Paul denies that of himself he has any capability to consider anything as his own. For Paul his sufficiency derives from God, and it is God who has made him sufficient to be a minister of the new covenant (6). The term "covenant" refers to the agreement initiated by God between God and Israel, whereby He would be their God and they would be His people. A hope for a "new covenant" is expressed by Jeremiah, a covenant to be written on the hearts of persons rather than on stone (Jer 31:31-34). At Qumran the Essenes also thought in terms of a new covenant and considered their community as sharing in it (e.g. CD 20:12; 6:19). Similarly the early church considered itself as sharing in the new covenant inaugurated by Christ, when it celebrated the Lord's Supper (cf. Mt 26:28; Mk 14:24; Lk 22:20; 1 Cor 11:25). Paul takes over this notion here from the early church and further specifies the new covenant as one based not on the letter but on the Spirit.

The exact meaning of this contrast between "letter" and "Spirit" has often been discussed. When taken in its present context, it appears as a polemical formulation by Paul against his opponents. Thus for Paul the "letter" seems to refer to his opponents' consideration of the covenant through Moses as still being in effect. For them the Scriptures from Moses could still be read as providing the way to salvation. For Paul, on the other hand, the Spirit points to the new action of God in Christ, whereby a new age and new covenant are introduced. Paul then adds his own theological judgment that "the letter kills." The Scriptures from Moses contain within them the demands of the Law which persons cannot fulfill of themselves. He further adds that "the Spirit gives life," God's grace which leads to life has been revealed in Christ.

MOSES AND HIS SCRIPTURES, CHRIST AND THE SPIRIT.
2 Cor 3:7-18.

[7]Now if the dispensation of death, carved in letters on stone, came with such splendor that the Israelites could not look at Moses' face because of its brightness, fading as this was, [8]will not the dispensation of the Spirit be attended with greater splendor? [9]For if there was splendor in the dispensation of condemnation, the dispensation of righteousness must far exceed it in splendor. [10]Indeed, in this case, what once had splendor has come to have no splendor at all, because of the splendor that surpasses it. [11]For if what faded away came with splendor, what is permanent must have much more splendor.

[12]Since we have such a hope, we are very bold, [13]not like Moses, who put a veil over his face so that the Israelites might not see the end of the fading splendor. [14]But their minds were hardened; for to this day, when

they read the old covenant, that same veil remains un-
lifted, because only through Christ is it taken away. ¹⁵Yes,
to this day whenever Moses is read a veil lies over their
minds; ¹⁶but when a man turns to the Lord the veil is
removed. ¹⁷Now the Lord is the Spirit, and where the
Spirit of the Lord is, there is freedom. ¹⁸And we all, with
unveiled face, beholding the glory of the Lord, are being
changed into his likeness from one degree of glory to
another; for this comes from the Lord who is the Spirit.

In this complex section Paul seems to enter into a lengthy
digression on the nature of the new covenant. Some interpreters in the past have suggested that the passage has no
relation to its context. However, recent studies have shown
that a more careful analysis of the polemical intent of this
section shows that it is an integral part of Paul's debate
with his opponents.

It seems clear that Paul has received a detailed report of
his opponents' position in this section. Their starting point
is Ex 34:29-30, and they interpret it in their own particular
way. Paul then takes care to rebut their position point by
point. In order to see the argument more clearly, it may be
helpful first to see the passage in full. The phrases at issue
from the passage will be italicized. Next, it seems best to
consider the position of the opponents. Then we shall see
the arguments of Paul. Ex 34:28-35 reads as follows:

"And he was there with the Lord forty days and
forty nights; he neither ate bread nor drank water.
And he *wrote upon the tables* the words of the
covenant, the ten commandments. When Moses
came down from Mount Sinai, with the two tables of
the testimony in his hand as he came down from the
mountain, *Moses* did not know that the skin of his
face shone because he had been talking with God.
And when Aaron and all the people of Israel saw
Moses, behold, the skin of his *face shone*, and they
were afraid to come near him. But Moses called to

them; and Aaron and all the leaders of the congregation returned to him, and Moses talked with them. And afterward all the people of Israel came near, and he gave them in commandment all that the Lord had spoken with him in Mount Sinai. And when Moses had finished speaking with them, *he put a veil on his face; but whenever Moses went in before the Lord to speak with him, he took the veil off*, until he came out; and when he came out, and told the people of Israel what he was commanded, the people of Israel saw the face of Moses, that the skin of *Moses' face shone;* and *Moses would put the veil upon his face again*, until he went in to speak with him."

With this as a Scriptural starting point, the opponents selected suitable phrases, expanded upon the text, and altered slightly the tenses of the verbs in order to present their interpretation of the meaning of the passage. For them, because Moses spoke with the Lord, his face shone in glory; and since the glory upon his face prevented the people from gazing upon him, Moses covered his face with a veil. For the opponents the veil seems to have covered not only the glory on Moses' face but also the meaning of his words. With the veil Moses has not only a hidden face but also hidden speech. Similarly the Scriptures from Moses have glory but also a veil to cover that glory; they have the words of Moses but the true meaning of them is hidden. When Moses turned to speak with the Lord, the veil was removed. Similarly when the follower of Moses is empowered by the Spirit, the veil from Scripture is removed so that one can behold the glory and so that one's own face can shine with glory. From this perspective, then, clearly the opponents of Paul would have claimed to possess the Spirit (cf. 2 Cor 11:4) and the divine glory and to be able to lead others to this same possession. Moses would have been the great example of the "divine man" and such accomplishments. Jesus would have been considered as a follower of Moses and another "divine man," while they considered themselves as apostles of this Jesus and as those commissioned to assist others to attain this glory.

In this context Paul's critique becomes more comprehensible. In a series of conditional sentences, he agrees with the Exodus account, places a negative theological judgment upon it and then by a question contrasts it to the present dispensation. He agrees, for example, that the ministry, which was engraved on stones, was inaugurated in glory (7). However, he adds that it was a ministry of death and that the glory was in the process of destruction. Both are judgments made from the perspective of faith that in Christ God has given life and has ended the covenant with Moses. Then Paul asks (8) how the ministry of the Spirit, in contrast, could not be in glory, i.e. the glory revealed in Christ (cf. 4:4). In the next conditional sentence, Paul identifies the old dispensation as a ministry of condemnation (9). By this reference Paul means that Moses provided the Scriptures but also the Law, which condemns a person by establishing God's requirements (cf. Rom 3:19-20). To it Paul contrasts the ministry of righteousness, the proclamation by himself as an apostle, that God has acted in the world to establish human beings in a right relation with himself. As a further thought Paul adds that the past glory was not truly glorious when compared with the surpassing glory of the present covenant (10). In a final, conditional sentence Paul contrasts the glory of the abolished dispensation with that of the remaining dispensation (11).

Next, Paul turns to the issue of the way in which his opponents and he view the Scriptures of Moses. Because of his hope to share in the glory of the new covenant Paul speaks boldly and does not place a veil upon his face as Moses did (12-13). He then adds, contrary to the view of Exodus and that of his opponents, that the real reason for the veil was so that the Israelites (i.e. his opponents; cf. 11:22) would not gaze upon the end of that which was perishing. Paul then judges that their minds were hardened in that they failed to understand that the covenant of Moses was meant to end. Next, Paul agrees with his opponents that there is a veil in the reading of the Scriptures from Moses (14). But he adds that the veil remains only as long as one fails to see that the old covenant has been destroyed by the coming of Christ and that the veil is placed not upon someone's face but upon the hearts of those who fail to believe in the new covenant inaugurated by Christ (15).

Paul then continues his argument in a passage that has long been disputed by exegetes. In accord with the understanding of the chapter so far, the following explanation seems preferable. Basing their position on Ex 34:34, his opponents claimed that whenever one turns to the Lord by inspired exegesis of the Scriptures, the veil is taken away (16). Paul then interprets the phrase "the Lord" in the Scripture quotation as a reference to the Spirit, the Spirit of the new covenant (17). Paul then adds that where the Spirit of the Lord is, there is freedom. For Paul this freedom is freedom from the Law but also from sin and from death (cf. Rom 6:15-23). Again Paul draws upon the claim of the opponents to have unveiled faces, to behold the glory, and to be transformed by a share in the glory, but modifies it drastically. In contrast to the special claims of these opponents for themselves, Paul claims that all Christians like Moses have unveiled faces and that they see the glory of the Lord but as in a mirror (18). When Paul is here quoting Scripture, he means by "the Lord" the God of the Old Testament as 4:1-4 will make clear. Thus, the "glory" of the Lord is Christ, who like Wisdom of old (cf. Wis 7:26) is a reflection or mirror of God, an image of God. According to Paul the Christian is being changed into this same image. The glory is present in Christ; the Spirit has been given to the Christian in accord with the new covenant; the Christian walks now in the hope of sharing in the glory of the final Kingdom (cf. vs. 12; 1 Cor 15:43).

APOSTOLATE AND KERYGMA.
2 Cor 4:1-6.

> **4** Therefore, having this ministry by the mercy of God, we do not lose heart. ²We have renounced disgraceful,

underhanded ways; we refuse to practice cunning or to
tamper with God's word, but by the open statement of
the truth we would commend ourselves to every man's
conscience in the sight of God.

³And even if our gospel is veiled, it is veiled only to
those who are perishing. ⁴In their case the god of this
world has blinded the minds of the unbelievers, to keep
them from seeing the light of the gospel of the glory of
Christ, who is the likeness of God. ⁵For what we preach is
not ourselves, but Jesus Christ as Lord, with ourselves
as your servants for Jesus' sake. ⁶For it is the God who
said, "Let light shine out of darkness," who has shone
in our hearts to give the light of the knowledge of the glory
of God in the face of Christ.

In this passage Paul continues to develop his view of his
apostolate in contrast to the view of his opponents. He does
so particularly by recourse to the gospel message. He opens
then by asserting that he has this ministry, his apostolate (1).
He then adds the qualification, which is so typical for Paul
and which sets him apart from his opponents, that this
apostolate is a result of mercy, namely, God's mercy (cf.
1 Cor 15:10; Gal 1:15-17). He continues with the statement
that he does not grow weary in his ministry. Then Paul
takes up the charges of his opponents against him, defends
himself against these charges, and also indirectly attacks
his opponents. He had been accused of exercising cunning
(12:16), of not showing the signs of a true apostle (cf. 11:13;
12:11-16), and of commending himself rather than being
commended by letters (3:1-3). Paul rejoins that he has
renounced shameful, hidden ways (2)—probably at the
point of conversion and call to his apostolate. Thus he
denies that he acts with cunning and hints that his opponents
do. He denies that he falsifies the gospel message and has
already stated that his opponents do (2:17). He agrees that
he commends himself but qualifies this statement in two
ways. First, he adds that it is by the manifestation of the
truth, i.e. the proclamation of the gospel, that he commends
himself to the moral judgment of persons; thereby he hints

that the opponents recommend themselves by their own achievements. Second, he adds that in commending himself he depends on God's call and commission rather than upon himself—as his opponents do.

Contrary to Paul's claim to manifest the truth, his opponents evidently charged that his gospel was veiled. The exact import of this charge is not clear. From the context it seems that Paul's weakness and lack of lustre are at issue (cf. 10:10); further, it seems that Paul's gospel is charged with not being able to produce a vision of God's glory, the light, such as the opponents claimed to provide for those who accepted their gospel and who engaged in inspired exegesis of the Scriptures as they did. Paul conditionally accepts this charge; the condition is that his gospel is veiled only for those who are in the process of destruction (3). Paul means here his opponents, Christians with a false gospel. He uses strong language to say that they are unbelievers and that "the god of this world" has blinded their minds (4). Paul has formulated the phrase "the god of this world" in analogy to "the God who said" in vs. 6 and by it refers to Satan (cf. 11:12-15); thereby he takes over the notion current in contemporary Judaism that Satan had usurped the authority of God and held the rule in this present age but that God would reassume his rule in the coming age. Paul then asserts that their lack of faith makes them unable to see the true light and the true glory. The light is that from the gospel message, and the glory is that which belongs to Christ. Paul further adds that the divine glory appears in Christ because he is the image of God. Thereby, Paul alludes to the Christology of the early church which is reflected in such hymns as Phil 2:6-11 and Col 1:15-20 (cf. also Jn 1:1,18; Heb 1:3). These hymns draw upon the Hellenistic Jewish tradition in which Wisdom is seen as preexistent and as the image of God (Wis 7:21-27). By applying this tradition to Christ, these hymns express his extraordinary dignity and the unique character of his relation to God. Paul expresses this belief in Christ and may well be rejecting a claim of his opponents that they too are "images of God."

As the basis for his understanding of his apostolate Paul then turns to the gospel message (5). It is simply that Christ Jesus is Lord (cf. 1 Cor 12:3; Rom 10:9). As the substance of Christian preaching it means for Paul that Jesus, as the Messiah who died and was raised for sins, presently rules from heaven. He is the sign of God's gracious love, the agent of atonement, and the victor over sin and death. His rule is presently in force, even though Satan is still allowed to work until the end of time when the powers of evil will be destroyed.

For Paul such a Christological confession determines the life of himself as a Christian. Just as in Phil 2:7-8 Paul can quote the hymn which acknowledges Jesus as taking the form of a servant and becoming obedient unto death, so Paul presents himself as a servant—a servant, first, of Christ (cf. Phil 1:1) and then in this context a servant of his community as an apostle. He then adds the motivation for his service—Jesus. Next, Paul adds that the basis for his apostolate is the new creation, which he has experienced in Christ (6). He alludes to the opening verses of Genesis ("God said, 'Let there be light'." Gen 1:3) and sees them fulfilled by his conversion, by the light in his heart. Again he is contrasting himself with his opponents, whose minds are hardened and whose hearts are veiled (3:14-15). He further sees as a new creation his apostolate which involves spreading the light that consists of the knowledge of God's glory. For Paul God's glory is not just his majesty but also his saving power. One attains to the knowledge of this glory not by ecstasy, as his opponents would suggest, but by faith that God's glory is present in the person of Christ.

THE APOSTLE'S SUFFERINGS AS EPIPHANY OF JESUS' LIFE AND SERVICE IN HOPE OF GOD'S GLORY.
2 Cor 4:7-15.

> [7]But we have this treasure in earthen vessels, to show that the transcendent power belongs to God and not to

us. [8]We are afflicted in every way, but not crushed; perplexed, but not driven to despair; [9]persecuted, but not forsaken; struck down, but not destroyed; [10]always carrying in the body the death of Jesus, so that the life of Jesus may also be manifested in our bodies. [11]For while we live we are always being given up to death for Jesus' sake, so that the life of Jesus may be manifested in our mortal flesh. [12]So death is at work in us, but life in you. [13]Since we have the same spirit of faith as he had who wrote, "I believed, and so I spoke," we too believe, and so we speak, [14]knowing that he who raised the Lord Jesus will raise us also with Jesus and bring us with you into his presence. [15]For it is all for your sake, so that as grace extends to more and more people it may increase thanksgiving, to the glory of God.

In this section Paul is rhetorically powerful as he uses images, figures of speech and paradoxes to make his point. Basically he is interested in showing here that his weakness and sufferings do not evidence a lack of apostolate on his part but rather manifest an apostolate which is derived from a suffering Lord and which has as its ultimate purpose the glory of God.

Paul opens this section with a striking image. The apostle carries the treasure of the gospel in earthen vessels (7). Paul has drawn upon the jewish wisdom tradition, in which Wisdom is considered as a treasure (Wis 7:14), in order to fashion the image of the gospel as a treasure (cf. Col 2:3). Similarly he turns to jewish tradition for the image of a pot or vessel. In the Old Testament the image functioned to show human beings as fragile, of little value before God (Ps 30:13; Jer 22:28), as instruments in the hands of God (Is 54:16-17). Specifically the image of "earthen" vessels or jars is used in a context of suffering as punishment for Israel's sins (cf. Is 30:14; Jer 19:1,11; Lam 4:2). For Paul the suffering is suffering as apostolic service. The point of the contrast then is the paradox between the inestimable value of the message and the suffering of the messenger.

For Paul this state of affairs is the result of God's purpose. God's intention is that the extraordinary character of the power may demonstrate that it is His power alone. By God's power Paul understands God's saving acts in history and specifically his saving act in the death of Jesus on the cross (cf. 1 Cor 1:18,24). Behind this statement there also lurks the claim of Paul's opponents that they possess divine power and can manifest it in their inspired exegesis and miracles; there is also an allusion to their attack on Paul that he is weak and fails to show any possession of divine power. For Paul, on the other hand, divine power is God's possession alone and not a human possession; and paradoxically it is present in his sufferings when he goes about preaching as an apostle.

To develop this point further, Paul turns to the rhetorical figure called the "list of trials" in vss. 8 and 9. In the Hellenistic world wandering philosophers would use this rhetorical form to stress the trials that a true sage must undergo and to emphasize the need for courage. Paul fills this form with language from jewish tradition, especially with the generalizing language of the Psalms which portrayed the sufferings of the righteous and their trust in God. In using this general terminology, Paul nevertheless has in mind the specific sufferings that he has endured as an apostle, such as attempted arrest (cf. 2 Cor 11:32) and persecution (cf. 1 Thess 1:6; 2:1). For him the list of trials is not intended to instill courage but to show that God's power is present precisely in the suffering and deliverance of his apostle.

Next, Paul turns to the paradox of the death and life of Jesus in his person. The issue is still the epiphany or manifestation of the divine presence in human life. For his opponents it was evident in the power of Christ and in their power. For Paul the divine presence was evident in the weakness of Jesus and in his weakness. Throughout these verses Paul uses the name Jesus rather than Christ or Lord in order to emphasize that the earthly Jesus who suffered death is the very same person who now rules as Lord. In vs. 10 Paul states that he bears the dying of Jesus in his body, that is, in his person as a whole (the jewish notion of the body, upon which Paul draws here, connotes the person as a whole and as an individual in history rather than a part of a person). The presupposition for this statement is that the dying of Jesus showed God's power. Thus the suffering of Paul, as one who is under the rule of Christ, shows that God's power was present in the dying of Jesus and is present in his own sufferings. Similarly Paul states that the purpose of bearing the dying of Jesus is to manifest the life of Jesus in his person. The resurrection of Jesus showed that God has inaugurated the new aeon, the new creation, the new life. Thus Paul's deliverance from suffering, because he does so as an apostle of the presently living and ruling Jesus, manifests the new life of Jesus in his person. Paul then reiterates this thought in the following verse. As a christian apostle he is subject to the perils of death. In using the term "being given up" to death Paul alludes to the early church formula on the death of Jesus (cf. Rom 8:32). That the apostle is given up to death because of Jesus indicates his faith and his willingness to conform himself to the pattern of existence found in Jesus. Paul adds this time that the life of Jesus is manifested in his mortal flesh, again the whole person considered from an external aspect as a limited creature in history.

In a brief sentence Paul then applies these thoughts to his apostolate (12). Death as a power derived from sin is active in his sufferings; but the life of the new age which is present in the proclamation of the gospel and in his own apostolic sufferings as a manifestation of the gospel is active among them, the recipients of the gospel, insofar as they accept the gospel and share in the new life (cf. Rom 6:1-11).

Paul then turns to the ultimate reason why he should act as an apostle and thus submit himself to these sufferings (13). He starts with a quotation from the psalmist in Ps 116:10: "I believed, and so I spoke." When Paul acknowledges that he too has believed, he need not specify the gospel as the different object of his faith. For him to speak is to preach the gospel (cf. 2:17).

Further, for Paul faith is not just a subjective attitude but contains an objective content. It consists in the knowledge that God has raised Jesus from the dead, that he will raise the apostle at the end of time to be with Jesus, and implicitly that he will also raise up Paul's Corinthian converts (14). Then as the final act God will present (to himself, understood) Jesus, his apostle, and his converts (cf. 1 Cor 15:20-24).

Thus Paul can conclude that the basis for all his actions, specifically his preaching and his suffering as an apostle, has been his converts (15). His ultimate purpose in attaining converts, he further specifies, is not to increase his own stature. His aim is that God's grace, which for Paul is God's gracious movement toward humanity in history and upon the cross, may spread to more people as the gospel is preached and accepted. Thereby, thanksgiving will be rendered to God as Christians acknowledge and respond to God's saving event in Jesus. In turn, this thanksgiving redounds to the glory of God in the sense of acknowledging and making known his glory rather than increasing it.

FOR THE APOSTLE ETERNAL GLORY RATHER THAN TEMPORAL ECSTASY.
2 Cor 4:16-5:10.

[16]So we do not lose heart. Though our outer nature is wasting away, our inner nature is being renewed every day. [17]For this slight momentary affliction is preparing for us an eternal weight of glory beyond all comparison, [18]because we look not to the things that are seen but to the things that are unseen; for the things that are seen are transient, but the things that are unseen are eternal. 5 For we know that if the earthly tent we live in is destroyed, we have a building from God, a house not made with hands, eternal in the heavens. [2]Here indeed we groan, and long to put on our heavenly dwelling, [3]so that by putting it on we may not be found naked. [4]For while we are still in this tent, we sigh with anxiety; not

that we would be unclothed, but that we would be
further clothed, so that what is mortal may be swallowed
up by life. [5]He who has prepared us for this very thing
is God, who has given us the Spirit as a guarantee.

[6]So we are always of good courage; we know that
while we are at home in the body we are away from the
Lord, [7]for we walk by faith, not by sight. [8]We are of
good courage, and we would rather be away from the
body and at home with the Lord. [9]So whether we are at
home or away, we make it our aim to please him. [10]For we
must all appear before the judgment seat of Christ, so
that each one may receive good or evil, according to what
he has done in the body.

This section has long been notoriously difficult for
interpreters of Paul because of a number of factors. First of
all, the passage seems to digress from the main point at issue.
Second, there are severe shifts in images: from an inner man
to a house to clothing to being at home. Third, there seems
to be a conflict between this passage and normal Pauline
eschatology. For example, in 1 Thessalonians 4 and 1
Corinthians 15 Paul awaits the second coming of Christ;
he expects to be alive at that time; and he looks forward to
being transformed into a person who will live eternally.
He does not reflect very much upon the situation of those
who have died already but merely says that they are asleep
(e.g. 1 Cor 15:6,18,20). Here in 2 Corinthians, however,
Paul seems to be more concerned about an intermediate
state, the state of those who have died before the end of the
world. Further, he seems to speak positively about this
state as a state of being "with the Lord." In addition Paul
seems to adopt here the language of Hellenism, which
distinguishes between a mortal body and an immortal soul.

A frequent explanation of this conflict between Paul's
customary position and his position here in 2 Corinthians
is that Paul has been somewhat led astray by his opponents.
According to this view, the topic for Paul and his opponents

is death. Paul then has taken over the language of his opponents and attempted to adapt it to his own views but has not been totally successful.

However, recent research on the views of the opponents has made possible an alternate hypothesis, which has the advantage of seeing a unity in the passage and of providing an explanation for the shift in images. According to this hypothesis the issue at hand between Paul and his opponents is not death at all but rather ecstasy, i.e. the mystic ascent of the soul to a vision of the divine which results in glorifying the soul. From the writings of contemporary Hellenized jewish authors, such as Philo of Alexandria, it is evident that such hopes were shared by some Jews of that period. As Jews who had come to believe in Christ, the opponents of Paul brought their heritage with them into their new faith. An important element in the opponents' Hellenized jewish heritage was the distinction between the body and soul. The body could be considered as the outer man, a house, clothing, or a place of exile. On the other hand, the soul could be considered as the inner man, a house, naked, or in exile. From this point of view when the soul is in the body, it is weighed down and has reason for groaning. Then the ascent of the soul to the divine realm by ecstasy can be described by various images. Negatively, that is from the viewpoint of the body, the ecstasy can be described as a wasting away of the outer man, as a destruction of the house, as putting off the clothing, or being in exile from the body. Positively from the viewpoint of the soul, the ecstasy is the attainment of glory and can be described as the making new of the inner man, as becoming a house of God, as putting on clothing, or as being at home.

As we shall see in the details of the commentary, Paul reacts sharply to this view. He adopts the language of his opponents but changes it to suit his position. For him glory will be attained at the parousia (the second coming of the Lord) rather than in ecstasy. Further, the sign of an apostle in this present life is suffering for the gospel rather than the glory of ecstasy. Finally, ecstasy is acceptable to Paul as a gift of God, but far more important is pleasing the Lord in one's daily activity.

With the clause "So we do not lose heart" (16), Paul summarizes the preceding section and picks up again the theme of 4:1. He has the ministry of an apostle; he suffers but also experiences God's power in it; he hopes in his resurrection as the moment to share in glory; and thus he does not grow weary. Then Paul introduces the image of "the outer man" and "the inner man." These images were used by the contemporaries of Paul, both pagan and jewish, in philosophical and religious contexts, and the usage had a long history running back as far as Plato. The images were mainly used to distinguish the body from the soul or the body from the mind. The wasting away of the body could refer either to death or to ecstasy. In this case, the opponents of Paul used it to refer to ecstasy. Further, they considered this ecstatic ascent of the soul as a "making new" of the soul.

In this verse (16) Paul adopts the language of his opponents. However, he thinks in terms of the whole person rather than in terms of component parts. For him "the outer man" refers to the person as subject to suffering whereas "the inner man" refers to the person as open to God. The phrase means the same here as the term "the heart" in 4:6. It is the place in which God has shone the light of his Spirit. For Paul then the moment of "making new" was when the Spirit entered the person. Thus, when Paul suffers as an apostle, he is made new again or renewed each day in the sense that he receives the power from God to sustain himself in his ministry.

Paul's perspective then turns (17) to the contrast between the present and the parousia, this life and the life to come. For his opponents the present is a time of glory through ecstasy. For Paul it is a time of suffering, whereas the parousia is a time of glory. In this verse Paul plays upon his opponents' idea of the body as a "weight" for the soul by terming the resurrected body or glorified body as a "weight of glory." A further aid to this play upon words was the fact that in Hebrew the term for glory also means weight. Thus Paul can say in contrast to his opponents that according to God's surpassing gift his present, momentary tribulation will be followed by eternal glory. With this in mind Paul "looks to" or fixes his gaze not upon the things that belong to this aeon but upon the things that belong to the coming aeon (18). Paul offers as his reason for this attitude the typical jewish and early christian belief that the time allotted by God for this aeon was limited whereas the coming aeon was eternal.

As Paul begins ch. 5, he switches to the image of a house. For his opponents the body was considered as a house, which was "destroyed" in the moment of ecstasy; the soul too was considered as a house, which became "a house of God" in the moment of ecstasy. Paul, however, contradicts and corrects this view by his eschatological perspective. He alludes to typical early church belief when he begins "we know" (1). He continues with the view that if "our earthly house," the "tent," is destroyed at the parousia rather than in ecstasy, we shall have a house from God. It is not the soul as "a house of God" or dwelling for God in a moment of ecstasy as the opponents would suggest, rather it is a building from God, the eternal glory of the resurrected and transformed body, which is appropriately pictured as a house in heaven that is not made with hands.

In vss. 2 and 3 Paul alludes to his opponents' view that they "groan" while in the body and desire to "take off" the body in order that their soul might ascend "naked" to the ecstatic vision of God. Paul again corrects this view with an eschatological perspective. He agrees with the idea of groaning, but his groaning is for the parousia (cf. Rom 8:23). Further, the idea of nakedness at the parousia is not attractive to Paul since the whole person (not just the soul) should have been clothed with or should have "put on" Christ (Gal 3:27) at baptism if he or she is to rejoice at the second coming of the Lord. This second coming will be the moment at which Paul will be transformed and share in the glory of the resurrection; in two images he will have his heavenly dwelling or receive his garment of glory in addition to the garment, which is Christ. From this perspective then Paul mixes his metaphors and says—in a more literal translation—that he too groans since he longs to put on in *addition* his heavenly dwelling, in the assurance that since he has already put on Christ, he will not be found naked.

With vs. 4 Paul now drops the image of the building and focuses on the image of clothing. He agrees with his opponents that those who are in the tent, the body, are weighed down and groan. But again he corrects their view. He does not groan to take off his body by means of an ecstatic ascent of the soul, but he groans for the moment of the parousia when he will put on in addition to Christ his glorious body. Then what is perishable or mortal, the human being, will be transformed by sharing in eternal life. For the notion of transformation Paul uses the image of death "being swallowed up" by life (cf. 1 Cor 15:54 where death is swallowed up by victory). Then in contrast to his opponents' emphasis on their own achievement Paul stresses (5) that the one who has prepared him for this final transformation is none other than God himself. He has prepared him for it by already giving the Spirit as the "guarantee." Perhaps a better translation than "guarantee" for the Hebrew term (*arrabōn*) used here in transliteration by Paul is the translation "first installment," since the term refers to that which is a part of and guarantee of the whole.

In this next section (6–10) Paul switches to the image of being "at home" or "away from home." The issue is the same. The opponents claim to be courageous; they consider life in the body as the soul's exile from God. Through the form in the soul they thus boldly seek to be with God by the ecstatic vision of God. Again Paul corrects their view by stressing his eschatological perspective and by relativizing the value of their ecstatic experiences.

Paul begins at first (6) positively and affirms that he too is always courageous. He acknowledges in the language of his opponents that earthly existence is separation from the Lord. He then adds the corrective that during our earthly existence we conduct our lives in the light of faith and not by means of a "form" (rather than "sight") within our souls (7).

Paul then adopts the language and agrees with the pref-
erence of his opponents to be "with the Lord" (8). For them
it is an ecstatic ascent of the soul from the body. Only the
soul could have this experience. For Paul it is a visionary
experience of the person. Paul is not clear about nor particularly concerned with the how of it. Here he can speak of
the experience as being "out of the body." Later in 12:2 and
3 he will discuss visionary experiences in relation to himself
but repeats that whether they are "in the body" or "out of
the body" he does not know; only God knows. In other
words, Paul denies a view which would see the person as
composed of the two parts—a body of lesser value and a soul
of greater value, which alone could have a vision of God.
For him the person is one, indivisible whole. In using the
language of his opponents, Paul seems at first glance to
adopt the dualistic framework of his opponents. However,
his correctives in 12:2 and 3 show that he has not, since a
dualistic position could never allow the possibility of a
vision "in the body." It is probably Paul's jewish idea that
one aspect (rather than one part) of the person is spirit,
which allows him to come so close to this dualistic position.

Paul next (9) relativizes the importance of these experiences. For his opponents they are the essence of religious
life. For Paul more important than having or not having
such experiences is the matter of acting in accord with the
will of the Lord. In vs. 10 then Paul adds the reason for this
emphasis on the will of the Lord. All, both he and his
opponents, must appear before the judgment seat of Christ
at the parousia. There the matter for judgment will be not
their ecstatic experiences but rather their deeds in the
daily, bodily existence. The criterion for judgment will be
whether their actions as apostles were good or evil.

PAUL'S APOSTOLATE BASED ON FAITH IN
CHRIST RATHER THAN ON ECSTASY.
2 Cor 5:11-21.

[11]Therefore, knowing the fear of the Lord, we persuade
men; but what we are is known to God, and I hope it is

known also to your conscience. [12]We are not commending ourselves to you again but giving you cause to be proud of us, so that you may be able to answer those who pride themselves on a man's position and not on his heart. [13]For if we are beside ourselves, it is for God; if we are in our right mind, it is for you. [14]For the love of Christ controls us, because we are convinced that one has died for all; therefore all have died. [15]And he died for all, that those who live might live no longer for themselves but for him who for their sake died and was raised.

[16]From now on, therefore, we regard no one from a human point of view; even though we once regarded Christ from a human point of view, we regard him thus no longer. [17]Therefore, if any one is in Christ, he is a new creation; the old has passed away, behold, the new has come. [18]All this is from God, who through Christ reconciled us to himself and gave us the ministry of reconciliation; [19]that is, God was in Christ reconciling the world to himself, not counting their trespasses against them, and entrusting to us the message of reconciliation. [20]So we are ambassadors for Christ, God making his appeal through us. We beseech you on behalf of Christ, be reconciled to God. [21]For our sake he made him to be sin who knew no sin, so that in him we might become the righteousness of God.

Since Paul has already compared his views with those of his opponents on ecstasy, in this section he now draws out the implications of this contrast for the apostolate (11-13). Then he turns to the theological basis of apostolate, uncovers the views of his opponents and contrasts his understanding of that basis with theirs (14-17). Lastly, he concludes this section with an appeal to the Corinthians as an apostle to them (18-21).

Paul first summarizes his statement in vs. 10 that he must appear before the judgment seat of Christ by the clause "Therefore, knowing the fear of the Lord." By "the fear of the Lord" Paul does not mean a cringing emotion before a powerful deity but rather the Old Testament idea of an attitude of respect and confidence before the God of holiness and love. Since he must be judged for his actions as an apostle, he persuades persons. Behind this assertion by Paul there seems to lie the charge by his opponents that Paul is deceiving the Corinthians, preaching a false gospel, and in his apostolate using false means that would not withstand God's inspection (cf. 4:2). The further assertion by Paul that "what he is is known to God" refers to the presence of the Spirit in Paul's heart (cf. 5:5; 1:22; 1 Cor 2:10), who has made known and continues to make known to God the real motives of Paul in his ministry. Then Paul expresses his hope that the true motives and the true nature of his apostolate have been made known to the Corinthians when he first preached to them and are still known to them. Again Paul probably means that it is the Spirit which has enabled the Corinthians to judge correctly Paul's true motives.

In vs. 12 Paul ironically recalls the charge in 3:1 that he commends himself. Without really granting that he does in fact commend himself Paul states that he is rather giving to the Corinthians an occasion to boast of him to his opponents. For Paul the term "boast" is of great significance. He charges his opponents with boasting in their own accomplishments. For Paul it is impossible that a human being should boast of his accomplishments before God. He does allow, on the other hand, that a person may boast of God's accomplishments for human beings. Thus Paul offers the Corinthians the opportunity to boast that God has called Paul to be an apostle and has sent him to be an apostle for them. He offers them the possibility of judging him according to God's standards and seeing that he is a true apostle. Paul concludes by characterizing his opponents as those who boast in the face, meaning their attainment of ecstasy, rather than in the heart, which is the change effected by God's Spirit within a person. In other words, they judge the value of a person by the wrong standards.

He concludes this section and summarizes the issues when he says that if he has had visionary experiences, they are moments of intimacy between God and himself; and if he speaks in a rational manner, it is that they may receive more fully the benefits of his apostolate (13).

In vss. 14-17 Paul turns directly to the basis of this reasonable apostolate. In vss. 18-21 he will make explicit its effects upon the Corinthians. As the cause for his apostolate Paul states (14) that it is Christ's love for him that controls him ever since he came to the decision of faith to accept the christian proclamation of the death and resurrection of Christ. This very message, with its two elements of death and resurrection, structures much of the remaining section. As a summary of the christian proclamation Paul first quotes the early credal formulation "one has died for all" (cf. 1 Cor 15:3; Mk 14:25), which signifies the salvific value of Christ's death. Paul then adds his own interpretation of the meaning of Christ's death when he states that "therefore all have died." He seems to mean here that all have died in the sense that the old aeon has passed away for all and that the possibility of a new existence is offered to all, although not everyone may seize the opportunity. Thus in vs. 15, as he turns to the theme of resurrection and its correlate life, he uses the more restrictive term "those who live" rather than "all." Those then who live, those who accept the Christian message, "no longer live for themselves but for him who for their sake died and was raised." Implicit in this sentence is the charge by Paul that his opponents who boast in their own accomplishments, in their own ecstasies, are living for themselves rather than for Christ. There is also implicit in this sentence the challenge to the Corinthians to judge correctly.

Paul then spells out the implications of his faith in the death and resurrection of Christ. First, because of his faith in the death of Christ he no longer judges anyone by merely human standards (16). When Paul uses the phrase "from now on," he refers to the eschatological moment of the death on the cross, that is, the change from the past aeon to the present (now) aeon, and also to his acceptance in faith of the preached message of Christ's death on the cross as an eschatological event. Again implicit in the sentence is the charge by Paul that his opponents are using merely human standards. Finally, Paul takes the case of Christ as a supreme example of the general proposition. For the moment he grants hypothetically that he might have judged Christ by merely human standards—as, he wants to say, his opponents continue to do so with their belief in a merely wonder-working Christ, who was filled with the Spirit. However, Paul distances himself from this view of Christ when he says that "we regard him thus no longer." Paul's faith is in Christ crucified and risen.

Paul then turns (17) to the implications of faith in the resurrection. One who believes in Christ and thus is within the realm of Christ's rule is a "new creation." With this phrase a "new creation" Paul draws upon jewish tradition, which saw no better way to express God's saving activity than to compare it to creation. His saving act in Christ was a new creation. In contrast to his opponents, who saw Christ as one more person in a long line of spiritual persons and events, Paul wants to stress the absolute change in the world that has occurred by Christ's death and resurrection. Thus he continues that "the old has passed away" and that "the new has come."

If this is the basis of Paul's apostolate in contrast with that of his opponents, then Paul now turns to the Corinthians and his mission to them from God. The theme that runs through these verses (18-21) is that of reconciliation, which is particularly appropriate to the situation. Paul begins by stating that the events recorded in vss. 14-17 all come from God as their ultimate origin. He then uses the metaphor of reconciliation to speak of God's saving event (cf. also Rom 5:10; Eph 2:16; Col 1:20-21). In itself this metaphor does not refer to a change of sentiments on the part of people or on the part of God. It refers to a change in the objective situation, in the relationship between humanity and God, which is the end of a relationship of enmity and its replacement with one of peace and good will. Paul particularly stresses two elements in this change: the initiative of God and the intermediation of Christ. Thus the relationship of enmity, which exists between humanity and God, is changed by the initiative of God, who accepted the death of his son as satisfying his wrath against sin and also as showing his love for persons (18). The moment of reconciliation was the moment of the cross but also the moment of Paul's acceptance in faith of the message of the cross. The latter was the same moment for Paul in which he received the ministry of reconciliation. For Paul his own work as an apostle fits within God's work. Reconciliation to God through the gospel and thus implicitly in this context to Paul as the apostle of the true gospel are part of God's ongoing work.

It seems probable that Paul then quotes a pre-existing formulation (19), perhaps a fragment from a hymn, as the general statement on reconciliation. "God was reconciling the world to himself through Christ," i.e. all of humanity. He did so by "not counting their trespasses against them." The language here is judicial or forensic. By not counting their sins against them God was equivalently offering forgiveness to humanity and the possibility of reconciliation. This possibility was seized by faith. Paul continues that those who have accepted this possibility have received the message of reconciliation. Again announcement of the gospel is seen as a necessary consequence and complement of the cross. In vs. 20 we find the key to this section (18-21). Paul appeals to the Corinthians to be reconciled to God, to accept again the gospel which they previously received and thus to share again in God's saving event. To accept the true gospel means also to accept Paul as an authentic apostle of it, as an ambassador of Christ through whom God speaks, and thus to be reconciled with him. Paul concludes with a sentence (21) that climaxes his argument and seems to be a formula that he expects would be familiar to the Corinthians. God made Christ sin in the sense that he placed him within the control of or within the realm of sin considered as a cosmic power. God's act in Christ's death is the act whereby he shows himself as a righteous God, as one who is faithful to himself and as one who saves his people. The death of Christ is seen then as an act of divine power by which God restores his sovereignty over the world. Those who accept Christ in faith are thus delivered from the evil powers of this world, such as sin, and enter into the control or within the realm of Christ and thus become those who manifest that God is righteous.

CALL TO RECONCILIATION.
2 Cor 6:1-10.

6 Working together with him, then, we entreat you not to accept the grace of God in vain. [2]For he says,
"At the acceptable time I have listened to you,
and helped you on the day of salvation."
Behold, now is the acceptable time; behold, now is the day of salvation. [3]We put no obstacle in any one's way, so that no fault may be found with our ministry, [4]but as servants of God we commend ourselves in every way: through great endurance, in afflictions, hardships, calamities, [5]beatings, imprisonments, tumults, labors, watching, hunger; [6]by purity, knowledge, forbearance, kindness, the Holy Spirit, genuine love, [7]truthful speech, and the power of God; with the weapons of righteousness for the right hand and for the left; [8]in honor and dishonor, in ill repute and good repute. We are treated as impostors, and yet are true; [9]as unknown, and yet well known; as dying, and behold, we live; as punished, and yet not killed; [10]as sorrowful, yet always rejoicing; as poor, yet making many rich; as having nothing, and yet possessing everything.

In his letters Paul often concludes his exposition with an exhortation, a moral exhortation. As part of the moral exhortation of Galatians he also uses a catalogue of vices and virtues (Gal 5:16-26), those actions to be avoided and those to be performed by Paul's converts. Here in 2 Corinthians the situation is different. Paul concludes his letter with an exhortation to the Corinthians to be reconciled to himself as their apostle. Instead of setting forth standards for his converts, Paul sets forth the standards for his own actions, standards by which he can be recognized as an apostle. As an apostle he "works together with God" in that he participates in God's great work in Jesus Christ (1). For Paul "the grace of God" is this saving event in Jesus Christ rather than a series of gracious interventions on God's part. However, for Paul that saving event is made present in his preaching. Thus Paul can appeal to his Corinthians "not to have received the grace of God in vain." They received the grace when they first accepted the gospel. They will have received it in vain, if they now reject the true gospel for a false gospel.

Paul then borrows the text of Is 49:8 as it was rendered in the Septuagint (2). There the passage referred to God's aid for his servant Israel. The passage may well have been used in the early church to show that the scripture was fulfilled in God's salvation of his servant Christ. For Paul the quotation is used to show that the saving moment is present in his preaching. His preaching is indeed part of the very saving act that he proclaims. His claim not to give offense is clearly a thrust against his opponents' charges (3). Further, it is noteworthy that Paul's concern is not to avoid censure of himself but censure of his ministry; his task rather than his person is his concern.

Next, he takes up again the charge that he commends himself since he produces neither letter of recommendation, wonders, or ecstasies (4). He denies that he simply commends himself but admits that he commends himself as a servant of God. Instead of catalogues of vices and virtues,

Paul presents catalogues of his own trials and then of virtues, both of which are highly rhetorical and lyrical in Greek. These type of catalogues, were well known in antiquity in both pagan and jewish circles. Paul may well have used them as part of his instructions to converts and fellow workers before incorporating them into his letters. Study of the content in these catalogues reveals that some of the phrases are stereotyped, some are polemical, and some have an echo in Paul's life.

As one considers the catalogue of trials, one notes the opening phrase "through great endurance"(4) and then the three sets of three hardships (vss. 4-5; cf. 11:23,27): those in general (afflictions, hardships, calamities), those from other people (beatings, imprisonments, tumults), those of a more personal nature (labors, watching, hunger). The phrases are very general. Perhaps it is more important to consider the function of this catalogue than to relate its contents to specific events in the life of Paul. Whereas his opponents would recommend themselves by a list of accomplishments, Paul presents himself by means of his sufferings since he preaches a crucified Christ who now reigns. He exhorts the Corinthians then not to avoid certain vices but to recognize his sufferings, to acknowledge him as an apostle, and thus to accept Christ crucified whom he preaches.

Paul turns then to the catalogue of virtues. He first (6) presents two sets of two virtues (purity, knowledge, forebearance, kindness) without any connectives as was the customary practice in such catalogues; these virtues are of a general nature. Paul then (6-7) breaks the pattern by introducing two sets of two modified terms in a chiastic structure, that is, a structure resembling an "x" in which the first and fourth and second and third terms are related. In this more emphatic structure we see the more specific points at issue in the letter. Paul asserts that his apostolic activity is by the Holy Spirit and by the power of God, contrary to the charges of his opponents concerning his lack of spirit and his weakness. Further, Paul states his genuine love and truthful speech, contrary to charges of craftiness and deception.

By means of phraseology that is appropriate to a catalogue of virtues ("with the weapons of righteousness for the right hand and for the left"), Paul then (7-8) turns to the circumstances of his apostolic ministry. The use here of antithesis and again a chiastic structure show the importance and specific nature of these terms. "Honor" and "good repute" signify the Corinthians' first reception of him; "dishonor" and "ill-repute" mark his opponents' estimation of him.

Finally, as the climax to this apology in miniature Paul turns to a series of seven paradoxical assertions, which contrast appearance with reality in the life of an apostle. Although considered to be a deceiver, he speaks the truth (8; cf. 3:12; 4:2). Although he is unrecognized as an apostle by some, he is so recognized by others (9; cf. 11:5-6). The power of a crucified and risen Christ is shown in the paradox of his suffering and yet deliverance. He seems to be dying but lives, to be punished but not put to death, to be saddened but always rejoicing (10; cf. 4:8-12). Lastly, though he is considered by the opponents to be spiritually poor and to have no spiritual power, Paul asserts that as Christ's apostle he enriches many with the wealth of the gospel and possesses all things in acknowledging Christ.

FINAL APPEAL.
2 Cor 6:11-13.

> [11]Our mouth is open to you, Corinthians; our heart is wide. [12]You are not restricted by us, but you are restricted in your own affections. [13]In return—I speak as to children—widen your hearts also.

In closing this "Letter of Defense" Paul invites the Corinthians to show a return of affection to him (6:11-13), a plea that is continued in 7:2-4. As we shall discuss shortly, the passage 6:14-7:1 seems to be a non-Pauline fragment that was inserted into our present 2 Corinthians at a later date by an editor.

Paul pours forth his emotion now directly to the Corinthians and reveals his own passionate nature when he is concerned with the cause of Christ. He proclaims that his mouth is open to speak the truth to them, that his heart as the seat of emotions is wide open to them, and that they have in no way been restricted to a narrow part of his affections (11-12). In return he appeals to them as his children, as those whom he has fathered by bringing them the gospel (cf. 1 Cor 4:14-15), to receive him in the same way (13).

APPEAL TO AVOID UNBELIEVERS.
2 Cor 6:14-7:1.

> [14]Do not be mismated with unbelievers. For what partnership have righteousness and iniquity? Or what fellowship has light with darkness? [15]What accord has Christ with Belial? Or what has a believer in common with an unbeliever? [16]What agreement has the temple of God with idols? For we are the temple of the living God; as God said,
> "I will live in them and move among them,
> and I will be their God,
> and they shall be my people.
> [17]Therefore come out from them, and be separate from them, says the Lord,
> and touch nothing unclean;
> then I will welcome you,
> [18]and I will be a father to you,
> and you shall be my sons and daughters,
> says the Lord Almighty."
> 7 Since we have these promises, beloved, let us cleanse ourselves from every defilement of body and spirit, and make holiness perfect in the fear of God.

Scholars have long noted the awkwardness of this passage in its present position. More recently a number of scholars have become convinced that the passage was not written by Paul. The arguments for this view are briefly as follows. First, the passage interrupts its context, which would flow more smoothly without it. Secondly, the passage contains vocabulary not elsewhere used by Paul, such as, the use of the name "Beliar" for Satan. Thirdly, the passage contains terms used elsewhere by Paul but used here in a sense very different from that of Paul. For example, Paul would speak of the flesh as that within a person which opposes the will of God but would not speak of "cleansing a defilement of the flesh" ("body" in the translation). Thus, it seems likely that the final editor has taken this non-Pauline fragment and inserted it here. The fragment shows some similarities to the Qumran literature and was probably originally composed by jewish Christians. The later editor evidently considered this section of exhortation in Paul's letter as an appropriate place to insert the passage, although thereby he mixes apostolic exhortation with moral exhortation. Presumably, the editor inserted the fragment because of a real concern on his part that Christians should not mingle with unbelievers but should act morally.

The author begins with an appeal that believers should not be associated with unbelievers (14). He uses the image of being "yoked together," which may refer to marriage but more probably to association with unbelievers (cf. Paul, who in 1 Cor 5:9-10 allows association with unbelievers as a necessity of life in the world). The author then applies this appeal in a series of rhetorical questions. The contrast between righteousness and iniquity is familiar from the OT. The contrast between light and darkness as distinguishing two groups within humanity rather than two ethical ways of living recalls the writings from Qumran (cf. the War Scroll). Further, the name Beliar in the contrast between Christ and Beliar (15) is a variation of the name Belial, which is found frequently at Qumran as the name of Satan. However, the presence of the contrast between Christ and Beliar makes it clear that only a Christian and not an Essene at Qumran could have composed this fragment. After a contrast between believer and unbeliever, the author concludes with a contrast between the temple of God and idols (16). He then identifies the christian community as a temple of the living God. At Qumran the community was frequently pictured as the temple of God. Paul, on the other hand, prefers to speak of the individual as the temple of the Holy Spirit (cf. 1 Cor 3:16; 6:19-20). Here clearly the author refers to the community.

The author then quotes a series of passages from various books of the OT and strings them together. Such a procedure was used within contemporary Judaism as the Qumran writings show. The structure of the quotations is clear. An opening statement is followed by an exhortation and then the promise for those who heed the exhortation. For the christian author God's statements that he would dwell with his people, that he would be their God and that they would be his people (cf. Lev 26:11-12; Ezek 37:27) have been fulfilled in the christian community. Therefore, according to the author (17) the Lord now exhorts them to disassociate themselves from unbelievers (cf. Is 52:11). If the christian community heeds this exhortation, according to the christian author (18) God promises to receive them (cf. Ezek 20:34), to be a father to them (cf. 2 Sam 7:14), and to have them as his sons (cf. 2 Sam 7:8) and daughters. On the basis of these promises the author then exhorts his hearers to cleanliness from every moral defilement (7:1).

CONCLUSION OF THE "LETTER OF DEFENSE."
2 Cor 7:2-4.

> [2]Open your hearts to us; we have wronged no one, we have corrupted no one, we have taken advantage of no one. [3]I do not say this to condemn you, for I said before that you are in our hearts, to die together and to live

together. ⁴I have great confidence in you; I have great pride in you; I am filled with comfort. With all our affliction, I am overjoyed.

In antiquity a common editorial practice was to insert a fragment and then to resume the thread of the original composition by repeating the phrase or idea prior to the insertion. Mark's gospel, for example, uses this technique frequently. The final editor has in effect used this device by splitting the two Pauline imperatives in 6:13 and 7:2, which state the same thought.

In his original "Letter of Defense" Paul continues with his appeal to the Corinthians to make room for him in their hearts. He offers his last denial of the charges by his opponents; he has not wronged, corrupted, or taken advantage of anyone (2; cf. 12:17-18). The tone of optimism and hope for reconciliation is clear as Paul states that the purpose of his comments has not been condemnation of the Corinthians. Again he stresses his affection for the Corinthians; as their apostle he gives himself to them unreservedly whether in death or life (3). He has spoken openly to them always and especially in this letter (4) and is glad to boast of them and their acceptance of the gospel to others. So optimistic is he that this letter will resolve the problems between himself and the Corinthians that Paul concludes with his expression of God's comfort to him and his joy in the midst of all tribulation, especially this tribulation. The original letter would have concluded with Paul's farewell blessing. Unfortunately, as chs. 10-13 demonstrate, Paul's difficulties with the turbulent Corinthians were by no means at an end.

NARRATIVE RESUMED:
PAUL'S JOY AT THE RETURN OF TITUS.
2 Cor 7:5-7.

⁵For even when we came into Macedonia, our bodies had no rest but we were afflicted at every turn—fighting

without and fear within. ⁶But God, who comforts the downcast, comforted us by the coming of Titus, ⁷and not only by his coming but also by the comfort with which he was comforted in you, as he told us of your longing, your mourning, your zeal for me, so that I rejoiced still more.

In this section Paul concludes his "Letter of Reconciliation." We return here to the narrative of 2:13, Paul's departure from Troas and entrance into Macedonia, which the editor had interrupted. At 2:13 the editor inserted the section 2:14-7:4 to show the triumphant spread of the gospel into Macedonia. He has skillfully woven 7:4 and 7:5-16 together to show further God's comfort and joy to Paul in preaching the gospel even in the midst of affliction.

In Macedonia Paul found grave difficulties (5). There is also no indication that the difficulties had abated as Paul was writing this letter. When he says that his "flesh" has found no relief, Paul refers simply to himself, the person, rather than the more theological sense of the "flesh" as the person turned away from God. The afflictions included "fighting without and fear within." Although no specific cities in Macedonia are mentioned (cf. Acts 20:1-6), one may well suspect that such a city as Philippi was intended for we know that Paul had a christian community there and we also know that there were serious difficulties in that community because of other missionaries (cf. Phil 3:2-21). The "fighting without" may well refer to controversies with other missionaries and civil authorities: the "fear within" may refer to anxiety over his communities as well as over his personal safety.

As part of his driving force, Paul possesses a firm belief in a God who comforts the humiliated or downcast (cf. Is 49:13). For Paul God's comforting of him in his affliction is part of God's total messianic comforting of his people (6). Paul then sees the return of Titus as part of God's comforting of him and this for two reasons: first, the return of a co-worker; and second, the news from Corinth which he brought. Evidently Paul and Titus had previously arranged some plan as to where and when they would meet in Macedonia. It is clear that as a co-worker in the gospel Titus had shared Paul's concern for the Corinthians and feared the loss of this community from the gospel which Paul preached. Paul is delighted to know that God has comforted Titus by showing him the steadfastness of the Corinthians in the true gospel (7). Further, Paul considers himself comforted by God to know that the Corinthians long to see him again, that they are saddened at the conflict and division which arose, and that they are determined to have him as their apostle. Thus Titus has brought the message of reconciliation from the Corinthians, which causes joy to Paul. Even more he has brought the message of their eagerness for Paul, which brings him greater joy. In these lines Paul shows that he is passionately involved as a person and that as an apostle he is not free from emotional upheavals.

THE SADNESS OF THE COMMUNITY
AT THE LETTER.
2 Cor 7:8-13.

> [8]For even if I made you sorry with my letter, I do not regret it (though I did regret it), for I see that that letter grieved you, though only for a while. [9]As it is, I rejoice, not because you were grieved, but because you were grieved into repenting; for you felt a godly grief, so that you suffered no loss through us. [10]For godly grief produces a repentance that leads to salvation and brings no regret, but worldly grief produces death. [11]For see what earnestness this godly grief has produced in you, what eagerness to clear yourselves, what indignation, what alarm, what longing, what zeal, what punishment! At every point you have proved yourselves guiltless in the matter.
>
> [12]So although I wrote to you, it was not on account of the one who did the wrong, nor on account of the one who

suffered the wrong, but in order that your zeal for us might be revealed to you in the sight of God. [13]Therefore we are comforted.

In 2:1-11 Paul had written about the sadness caused by his "intermediate" visit to Corinth. Here (8) he turns to the sadness caused by his letter after the visit. It has been suggested in the past that the letter referred to was the lost letter mentioned in 1 Cor 5:9 or 1 Corinthians or even another lost letter. It seems more probable that the letter referred to here and at 2 Cor 2:4 (the "Letter of Tears") is substantially contained in chs. 10-13.

In this section Paul expresses himself in a very delicate and thus very complex manner in order to complete the process of reconciliation. It is clear that Titus has reported the great sadness of the Corinthians at Paul's "Letter of Tears." It seems likely in addition that Titus also communicated their regret that Paul considered it necessary to write such a letter.

In response, Paul wants to express his joy at the outcome of the letter. Further, because of the outcome and also because of his concern for others he wants to avoid the unqualified statements—"I regret sending the letter" or "I rejoice that I caused you sadness." Thus, he is led to a somewhat involved mode of expression. He begins by asserting that he has no regret, even if it is indeed true that he has caused sadness by the letter (8). Then he states that if in the past he did regret, he now rejoices (9). Clearly Paul hints that sometime after writing the letter, he regretted writing it because he feared that it would hurt the Corinthians. In a remark, which is best taken as a parenthesis to Paul's past regret, Paul admits that there was a basis for his regret; he did in fact hurt the Corinthians. Then he adds the further qualification—the hurt was only for a short while, i.e. until the time of reconciliation. Finally, Paul adds the further modification on his joy. He rejoices not simply that they were saddened but that their sadness resulted in repentance. In the light of this analysis a better translation of vss. 8-9 might be as follows: "If indeed I saddened you by my letter, I have no regret. If indeed I did regret (I see that that letter did sadden you, if only for a while), I now rejoice—not that you were caused sadness but that your sadness led to repentance."

The repentance about which Paul speaks here is not the repentance which is the conversion from paganism to Christianity. Rather, it is the decision and change of a Christian who has turned away from and now returns to the way of salvation. It is striking that Paul does not often use this term. In Rom 2:4 he does employ it to refer to conversion to Christianity; usually he prefers to speak of the death of the "old man." In 2 Cor 12:21 the repentance probably also refers to that of Christians. While the absence of this term in Paul is not entirely clear, it may be that Paul avoided it because it did not stress sufficiently God's action in salvation.

Paul then adds that it was in accord with God's will that the Corinthians should experience this sadness. God's purpose in allowing this sadness according to Paul was that they might suffer no loss on account of him. The loss considered is the loss of the gospel and thus of salvation if Paul had failed to act with his apostolic authority and if the Corinthians had rejected Paul as their apostle of the true gospel. As vs. 10 makes clear, such a sadness brings about a repentance unto salvation, a result that is not to be regretted. Contrary to such sadness which is in accord with God's will is the sadness of the world; its result is death. By the term "the world" Paul means creation insofar as it is turned away from God. Thus, in this sense "the world" leads to condemnation and loss of salvation, which is death. Therefore, Paul makes clear to the Corinthians the depth of the issues involved in the past conflict and in his past letter. A sadness on their part, which was merely embitterment, anger, or despondency and which resulted in their rejection of Paul and his gospel, would have led to condemnation (cf. 11:12-15).

Fortunately the sadness which the Corinthians experienced was according to God's will rather than from the world. Thus Paul can point in a rhetorically strong verse (11) to the signs that indicate the true nature of their sadness. They are earnest or serious in the matter. They defend themselves—probably against Paul's accusation that they have accepted the false prophets. They are indignant— probably at the false apostles and the Corinthians who have taken their side against Paul. They are fearful probably in the sense that they recognize God's authority behind Paul's apostolate. They are longing evidently to see Paul. They are zealous for the gospel and for Paul as their apostle. And lastly they have inflicted punishment—probably upon the members of the community who decided for the opposing apostles rather than for Paul. After this list Paul can conclude that the Corinthians have shown that they are now innocent in the matter. Since they have turned away from the opposing apostles, the necessary basis for restoring harmony between the apostle and his community is established.

Paul concluded this section by returning to the purpose of his letter. It was not for the sake of punishment of the wrongdoer or vindication of himself that Paul wrote but rather for the sake of the Corinthians themselves (12). Scholars have considered the reference to "the wrongdoer" as an allusion to an unknown member of the Corinthian community who somehow seriously insulted Paul during his "intermediate" visit to Corinth. Those who consider chs. 10-13 as a substantial portion of the "Letter of Tears" also consider that the letter omitted this incident or that the portion of the letter in which the incident was recounted has not been preserved. It seems more likely, however, that Paul is referring to those members of the Corinthian community who decided for the opposing apostles and thus against Paul during his "intermediate" visit. In chs. 10-13 Paul can refer to these opposing apostles as "anyone" (10:7) or "such a one" (10:11) or "the one who comes" (11:4), all in the singular. Similarly it seems that there were a number of persons within the Corinthian community, who decided to continue to accept the false apostles (cf. 13:2). Their number we cannot discern. However, it is clear from 2:6 that they were not in the majority. Just as Paul could designate the false apostles by such singular terms, so he refers to these formerly dissident Corinthians as "anyone" (2:5), "such a one" (2:6), or "the one who does wrong" (7:12). Evidently the Corinthians had punished the offenders, probably by exclusion from the community, and had considered the punishment in accord with Paul's own will, at least as implicitly stated in his letter (cf. 13:2,10). As Paul related, his purpose in writing the letter was for the Corinthians. Although even the majority had accepted the false apostles and their false gospel but had not rejected Paul and his gospel, Paul's confrontation with the Corinthians both in person and by letter made evident the impossiblity of this dual allegiance. Thereby the sincerity of their own desire to have Paul as their apostle and thus to remain within the true gospel was made clear to them. On this basis Paul finds his comfort: God has delivered him and his community from the threat to the gospel.

THE EXPERIENCE OF TITUS IN CORINTH.
2 Cor 7:13-16.

> And besides our own comfort we rejoiced still more at the joy of Titus, because his mind has been set at rest by you all. [14]For if I have expressed to him some pride in you, I was not put to shame; but just as everything we said to you was true, so our boasting before Titus has proved true. [15]And his heart goes out all the more to you, as he remembers the obedience of you all, and the fear and trembling with which you received him. [16]I rejoice, because I have perfect confidence in you.

Paul frequently includes his companions in his thoughts of thanksgiving, intercession, and joy. In this passage he turns to the special joy which the rejoicing of Titus has given him (13). When Paul mentions that the Corinthians have given rest to the spirit of Titus, he means simply the human spirit of Titus rather than the Holy Spirit. It is clear that Paul had some concern over how Titus would be received by the community. After all, Titus had been entrusted with the difficult mission of carrying the "Letter of Tears" to Corinth and of re-establishing Paul's apostolic authority. Paul adds that "if I boasted to him about you, I have not been put to shame" (14). It seems hardly likely that Paul boasted of the Corinthians prior to Titus' difficult mission. Possibly Paul had boasted of them on previous occasions or possibly Paul is merely adding a rhetorical flourish in the spirit of reconciliation. In any case, the verse also shows Paul's fear as Titus undertook his mission, a fear that the Corinthians might not return to him and might not rebuff those within the community who had decided for the false apostles. Paul then rejoices that his boasting to Titus has been shown true. Further, he associated the truth of his boasting with the truth of all that he has said to the Corinthians. Thereby, he seems to allude to the former accusation that he was crafty and deceptive (12:16).

Paul adds that Titus especially remembers affectionately the obedience of all the Corinthians, their reception of him, and their fear and trembling (15). The obedience of the Corinthians refers to their obedience to the gospel and to Paul as the authoritative apostle of the gospel. In the OT the attitude of fear and trembling is the appropriate human response to the presence of God. Thus for Paul here it is also the appropriate response to God's presence in the gospel and in his apostolic authority. Further, in accord with jewish notions of the time, as the delegate of Paul Titus was invested fully with Paul's apostolic authority. All of those Corinthians to whom Paul is presently writing had accepted Titus and thus the gospel. Therefore, while recalling the accusation that he lacked this quality (cf. 10:1,2), Paul can boast in his confidence and boldness toward them (16).

III. A LETTER OF RECOMMENDATION TO CORINTH FOR TITUS AND THE BRETHREN 2 COR 8

The two chapters 8 and 9 are written from different situations and to different audiences—Corinth and Achaia. Thus they were probably not written at the same time. Further, the "Letter of Reconciliation" (1:1-2:13; 7:5-16) seems to presuppose a different situation than that of ch. 8. The former was written immediately after Titus arrived and while the churches in Macedonia were still experiencing trials (7:5). The latter was written sometime later as Titus was departing for Corinth and after the trials for the churches had abated (8:2). Thus it seems that these originally independent letters were later collected and incorporated by the editor into our present 2 Corinthians.

In these two chapters (8 and 9) Paul discusses the collection which played an important role in his apostolic ministry in the 50's (cf. 1 Cor 16:1-4; Rom 15:25-32; Acts 24:17; cf. also Gal 2:10). Its purpose was not to provide public charity in all the churches; rather the collection was destined for Jerusalem. Its aim was not so much to provide for the needs of the Christian in Jerusalem as to recognize the special role which Jerusalem played in the history of salvation. The collection relates to the jewish expectation that in the last days, the period of God's intervention in history, the Gentiles would come to Jerusalem with gifts. From this perspective the purpose of the collection in Paul's mind was to manifest that the last days had indeed arrived in Christ, to symbolize the unity of the church which was composed of Jews and Gentiles, to show their equal status within the church, and to demonstrate the validity of the gospel without the law by the evidence of God's accomplishments through it.

THE EXAMPLE OF THE MACEDONIANS.
2 Cor 8:1-6.

> **8** We want you to know, brethren, about the grace of God which has been shown in the churches of Macedonia, ²for in a severe test of affliction, their abundance of joy and their extreme poverty have overflowed in a wealth of liberality on their part. ³For they gave according to their means, as I can testify, and beyond their means, of their own free will, ⁴begging us earnestly for the favor of taking part in the relief of the saints—⁵and this, not as we expected, but first they gave themselves to the Lord and to us by the will of God. ⁶Accordingly we have urged Titus that as he had already made a beginning, he should also complete among you this gracious work.

In ch. 8 Paul begins his appeal to the Corinthians by pointing to the example of the Macedonians (1). Although the churches are not specified more precisely than being in Macedonia, which was then a Roman province, we do know that at least Thessalonica and Philippi were Pauline communities within that province. Paul particularly points out that they were generous even in the midst of tribulation, which now seems to be past (2). Further, although Paul arranged the collection in his communities, he notes the eagerness and independence with which the Corinthians sought to participate in the collection (3-4).

Even beyond the question of its purpose, the collection for Paul is more than simply a donation of money. He uses religious language for the collection such as a grace, a fellowship, a ministry or service, a work of love for the saints. This language springs from Paul's conception that life and service within the community, daily actions and necessities, are not simply profane activities but are also part of the Christian's service of God and Christ. They are made possible by the grace of God, just as the collection was made possible by the grace of God. Indeed, for Paul it is God's grace that makes it possible for the Christian to love and serve within the community. Paul then continues (5) that the Macedonians have gone beyond his hopes. They have given not only money but also themselves.

Paul then gives the theological basis for their action. It is through the will of God that they participated in this collection and that they also dedicated themselves to Christ, the Lord. Further by participating in the collection they have also shown their commitment to Paul as their apostle. As a result of their example Paul has asked Titus to go again to Corinth (6). Titus had begun to organize the collection there on a previous occasion—probably during his visit with 1 Corinthians rather than when he brought the "Letter of Tears." The mission of Titus will now be to complete the collection. In the Greek text there is the extra word "too" ("he should also complete among you this gracious work too"), which may well hint at Titus' successful work in effecting reconciliation with the "Letter of Tears."

APPEAL FOR WHOLE-HEARTED PARTICIPATION. 2 Cor 8:7-15.

7Now as you excel in everything—in faith, in utterance, in knowledge, in all earnestness, and in your love for us— see that you excel in this gracious work also.

8I say this not as a command, but to prove by the earnestness of others that your love also is genuine. 9For you know the grace of our Lord Jesus Christ, that though he was rich, yet for your sake he became poor, so that by his poverty you might become rich. [10]And in this matter I give my advice; it is best for you now to complete what a year ago you began not only to do but to desire, [11]so that your readiness in desiring it may be matched by your completing it out of what you have. [12]For if the readiness is there, it is acceptable according to what a man has, not according to what he has not. [13]I do not mean that others should be eased and you burdened, [14]but that as a matter of equality your abundance at the present time should supply their want, so that their abundance may supply your want, that there may be equality. [15]As it is written, "He who gathered much had nothing over, and he who gathered little had no lack."

Paul begins his appeal to the Corinthians by pointing to their spiritual riches: their faith, speech, knowledge, and zeal (7). As a final example of their spiritual riches he mentions "your love for us." An alternate and preferable reading in the ancient manuscripts is "our love for you." Paul knows of the genuineness of his love for the Corinthians; on the other hand, the collection will test the genuineness of their love for him (cf. vs. 8). Since they possess all these gifts, Paul exhorts the Corinthians to share as well in this gift of grace, which is generosity in this collection. Paul then adds that he is not issuing a command on the basis of his apostolic authority. For him the collection is rather to be a free work of love, which symbolizes the unity of the church as a community. He would prefer that their love be no less than that of the Macedonians, and the example of the Macedonians provides a criterion for testing the reality of their love for him and their fellow Christians (8).

A better criterion, however, is offered in the story of Christ. He, although rich, became poor in order that they, though poor, might become rich (9). Paul refers here to the pre-existence of Christ in heaven and his possession there of divine riches. His incarnation then is considered as the surrender of these riches so that humanity could share in the spiritual riches of salvation (cf. Phil 2:6-11; Rom 15:3). Thus his poverty becomes the sign of his sending by the Father, which reaches its climax in his death on the cross. Christ then is the example to be imitated by the community in their relation with their fellow Christians. If he became poor in order to share his riches, then they too are to share their earthly riches as a sign of the genuineness of their love for their fellow Christians.

Paul then adds that he offers them his advice in this matter (10), since he is responsible for their christian existence (cf. 1 Cor 7:25,35 where Paul also distinguishes between a command of the Lord and advice that is best). According to Paul they should complete the collection; after all they had begun before the Macedonians. In response to their eager question, Paul had given instructions concerning the collection in 1 Cor 16:1-4. Paul adds that they began in the preceding year. It is likely that Paul was using the jewish calendar or the oriental-Julian calendar, which began the new year in the fall. If 1 Corinthians was written in the Eastertime (1 Cor 16:8) of 54, then this letter on the collection (2 Cor 8) would have been written at the latest in the summer of 55 and prior to the beginning of the new year in the fall. Then Paul adds a catching and appropriate inversion. He states that the Corinthians had begun to act and to will rather than vice versa as one would expect. He exhorts them then to complete the action since he presumes the will is still present and since he wants their action to be in accord with their will. Then Paul adds a principle (12) that is familiar in jewish and christian (cf. Lk 12:47-48) tradition. The readiness of will is more important than the amount. The gift is acceptable to God if one gives in proportion to one's possessions—no matter what the size of the amount.

Paul concludes this appeal by avoiding a possible misunderstanding. His aim in the collection is not to provide a one-sided relief for those in Jerusalem but distress for those in Corinth (13). Rather his concern is that their abundance should supply the needs of those in Jerusalem. Thus there will be equality. If the roles were reversed in the future, Paul would expect the same generosity from those in Jerusalem. As an example from the OT, Paul refers to the collection of manna in the desert when the Israelites by God's power all had the same amount (Ex 16:18). So too by God's grace the collection will effect equality.

RECOMMENDATIONS.
2 Cor 8:16-24.

> 16But thanks be to God who puts the same earnest care for you into the heart of Titus. 17For he not only accepted our appeal, but being himself very earnest he is going to you of his own accord. 18With him we are sending the brother who is famous among all the churches for his preaching of the gospel; 19and not only that, but he has been appointed by the churches to travel with us in this gracious work which we are carrying on, for the glory of the Lord and to show our good will. 20We intend that no one should blame us about this liberal gift which we are administering, 21for we aim at what is honorable not only in the Lord's sight but also in the sight of men. 22And with them we are sending our brother whom we have often tested and found earnest in many matters, but who is now more earnest than ever because of his great confidence in you. 23As for Titus, he is my partner and fellow worker in your service; and as for our brethren, they are messengers of the churches, the glory of Christ. 24So give proof, before the churches, of your love and of our boasting about you to these men.

After appealing to the Corinthians for the collection on the basis of the example of the Macedonians, Paul now recommends to them those who are appointed for this task. Thereby, he hopes to present them to the Corinthians and to ease their work. He begins by thanking God for giving Titus the same zeal as himself for the Corinthians (16).

After hearing Paul's request Titus was more zealous than Paul even hoped. He is leaving for Corinth not only because of the request of Paul but out of his own desire (17).

In addition to Titus Paul is sending two other Christians. Strangely, the names of these delegates are not given, although Paul customarily does give the names of his co-workers. Some scholars have suggested that Titus would have introduced the delegates by name when he read the letter to the Corinthians. However, since a letter of recommendation should normally mention the name of the person being recommended, it seems more probable that Paul included the names. A plausible hypothesis is that the final redactor of 2 Corinthians has removed the names of these delegates here (he has probably also removed the different names at 9:3 and 12:18).

The two Christians who accompanied Titus also seem to be of unequal importance. The first delegate is known in all the churches, presumably the churches of Macedonia, for his preaching of the gospel—perhaps as a missionary. He was appointed by the churches—again probably in Macedonia—to be a companion with Paul in the collection for Jerusalem (19). Paul shows the effects of the conflict with the opposing apostles in Corinth and their charge against him when he adds that he arranged for the appointment of church delegates so that he could not be accused of dishonesty in the gathering and transfer of the collection (20; cf. 12:16-18). As the basis for this arrangement Paul quotes loosely the Greek text of Prov 3:4 to show that as an apostle he is concerned not only with appearances before the Lord, who is the true judge, but also with appearances before persons, probably since an appearance of falsehood would hinder the spread of the gospel. The second delegate is one tested and approved by Paul (22). Paul's reference to this brother's confidence in the Corinthians may indicate his previous acquaintance with them or simply his reliance upon Paul's estimation of the Corinthians.

In short, elliptic sentences Paul then recommends these three emissaries to the Corinthians. Titus is placed first since he belongs to the small group of Paul's companions and co-workers in the gospel. Then Paul identifies the two brethren as messengers or apostles of the churches (the term is the same in Greek). Thereby, Paul draws upon the typical jewish understanding in which an "apostle" is an agent sent with the full power of the person sending him. However, there is a difference when this term is applied to these delegates and to Paul. Paul claims to have received his commission and authority directly from Christ and not through an intermediary such as the churches (cf. 1 Cor 15:4-7). All three emissaries are then identified as the "glory of Christ"; in this ministry of the collection they are ultimately witnesses and messengers of Christ. Paul concludes then with an appeal to the Corinthians (24) to receive these brethren in love and to show all the churches, which will know of their behavior, that Paul has been correct in boasting of their christian faith and life. Thus in this letter of recommendation Paul demonstrates his belief in the responsibility of one christian community to another. The action of one community is known to another and should serve as an example and spur to greater christian charity by the other.

IV. A LETTER OF RECOMMENDATION TO ACHAIA FOR THE BRETHREN. 2 COR 9:1-15.

A major portion of a second letter on the collection is preserved in ch. 9. This letter served as a letter of recommendation for some unnamed brethren to the churches in Achaia. Its purpose was to present the brethren to the communities, to ease their work in the collection, and to exhort the Achaians to generosity. Some scholars consider ch. 9 to be a continuation of ch. 8, although they note the overlap in content. It seems more likely that ch. 8 was written to Corinth and that sometime later in the summer of 55 ch. 9 was written to the churches in the Roman province of Achaia. Corinth was the largest city within this province, but it was not the only city in the province with a christian community (cf. Rom 16:1). The editor has placed the chapters in the correct order of composition probably because of the reference to Paul's coming from Macedonia to Achaia (4-5), which reference would indicate a later date, and probably because of the analogy with 1 Corinthians in which the collection is treated (1 Cor 16:1-4) before Paul's travel plans from Macedonia to his community (1 Cor 16:5-9).

RECOMMENDATION OF THE BRETHREN.
2 Cor 9:1-5.

9 Now it is superfluous for me to write to you about the offering for the saints, ²for I know your readiness, of which I boast about you to the people of Macedonia, saying that Achaia has been ready since last year; and your zeal has stirred up most of them. ³But I am sending the brethren so that our boasting about you may not prove vain in this case, so that you may be ready, as I said you would be; ⁴lest if some Macedonians come with me and find that you are not ready, we be humiliated—to say nothing of you—for being so confident. ⁵So I thought it necessary to urge the brethren to go on to you before me, and arrange in advance for this gift you have promised, so that it may be ready not as an exaction but as a willing gift.

In this letter Paul has no need to write to the Achaians about the reasons for the collection since they are sufficiently convinced of its value and are eager to participate in it (1). His task is to encourage them to complete the collection and to complete it generously. In ch. 8 Paul had used the generosity of the Macedonians to stir up the Corinthians. Here (2) he reminds the Achaians that in the past he has spurred on the Macedonians by their willingness. He had even said that the Achaians had been prepared since last year (2).

This exaggeration on the part of Paul—or, perhaps better, his readiness to see his communities in their best possible light—has obviously caused him some embarrassment already. In order to avoid further embarrassment, Paul is sending brethren to Achaia to complete the collection (3). Those who consider ch. 9 as a continuation of ch. 8 would see in this verse a further reference to Titus and/or the brethren of 8:17-24. It seems more probable that two new delegates are being dispatched. Again, presumably the names of these brethren were contained in the original letter and later removed by the final editor. Without the specific names the composite letter would have had a more general value and appeal. Paul's fear is that he will be further embarrassed if the Macedonians come with him to Achaia and find that his praise of the Achaians has been unjustified (4).

In a further, delicate parenthesis Paul suggests that the real embarrassment in the situation will not be to himself but to the Achaians. To avoid this situation, then, Paul has sent the brethren in advance to prepare the collection. As a further reason for their arrival Paul suggests that thereby the collection may be prepared as a gift of blessing rather than as an exaction demanded by Paul (5). By this term "willing gift" or "gift of blessing" Paul thinks that the gift should be generous (cf. 6), and that it should announce God's blessing (cf. 8). Surely by the term "exaction" Paul remembers here and alludes to the charges against him by his opponents in Corinth (12:17-18).

THE COLLECTION AND THE
UNITY OF THE CHURCH.
2 Cor 9:6-15.

> [6]The point is this: he who sows sparingly will also reap sparingly, and he who sows bountifully will also reap bountifully. [7]Each one must do as he has made up his mind, not reluctantly or under compulsion, for God loves a cheerful giver. [8]And God is able to provide you with every blessing in abundance, so that you may always have enough of everything and may provide in abundance for every good work. [9]As it is written,
>
> "He scatters abroad, he gives to the poor;
> his righteousness endures for ever."
>
> [10]He who supplies seed to the sower and bread for food will supply and multiply your resources and increase the harvest of your righteousness. [11]You will be enriched in every way for great generosity, which through us will

produce thanksgiving to God; [12]for the rendering of this service not only supplies the wants of the saints but also overflows in many thanksgivings to God. [13]Under the test of this service, you will glorify God by your obedience in acknowledging the gospel of Christ, and by the generosity of your contribution for them and for all others; [14]while they long for you and pray for you, because of the surpassing grace of God in you. [15]Thanks be to God for his inexpressible gift!

After recommending the brethren to the Achaians, Paul now turns to the collection itself. In this section Paul makes an appeal for generosity, relates the collection to christian life, and then treats the significance of the collection for the unity of the church.

In making this appeal for generosity Paul draws upon the image of the sower scattering seed, which image carries through this section. He first quotes a saying that seems to be a proverb, although no exact parallel is known (6). For Paul the proverb is of interest since it can be related to the collection and to God. God will reward in accord with one's generosity in life (cf. Gal 6:7). Paul then adds that each person is to give as he or she sees fit. The donation is to come from conviction rather than constraint (7). In support of this position Paul quotes Prov 22:8 on God's love for "a cheerful giver."

Next, Paul expands his view to the wider theological basis of this collection—the christian existence of the Achaians. He begins with God himself. As the source of every grace, God is both the basis and the example for the Corinthians in their generosity. Then Paul turns to a widespread notion at that time that a person should be self-satisfied, content, or "have enough," whether those material things be large or small. For Paul such a self-centered contentment would be unacceptable. He expresses his faith that God will abundantly provide his grace for the Achaians so that their contentment will enable them to transcend themselves and perform "every good work" for others (8).

For Paul God not only rewards the gift but also makes the action possible. As support for this view (9) he quotes scripture, Ps 111(112):9. The passage is appropriate since it continues the image of sowing seed as applied to the collection. When Paul quotes his "righteousness endures forever," he may have in mind the later jewish understanding of this term as almsgiving or he may have in mind the moral sense of an upright act. More probably, however, he intends here the more theological sense of the right relationship between God and a person, which has been established by God's act in Christ and is appropriated by the person through faith. Paul then continues the image of the seed and draws on biblical phrases (Is 55:10; Hos 10:12) to assure the Achaians that God will provide them with the means to participate in the collection and will give an increase to this action, which springs from their righteousness (10).

The last phrase "the harvest of your righteousness" or better "the fruits of your righteousness" allows Paul to turn his attention to the final theme in this section, the collection and the unity of the church. Paul recalls to the Corinthians that through the gospel they have been enriched in every way and are thus led to a sincerity or singleheartedness (rather than "generosity") that is bringing about thanksgiving to God (11). As the reason for the thanksgiving to God, Paul adds that the execution of this service, the collection, takes care of the needs of the Christians in Jerusalem, but it has the further effect of producing many thanksgivings to God (12). Clearly Paul intends thanksgiving to God by the Christians in Jerusalem for their generous gift, but he then turns to a deeper reason for thanksgiving by those in Jerusalem. The collection is to be considered a test of the true commitment in faith to the gospel of Christ by these gentile Christians from Paul's mission. The completion of the collection will show that they have passed the test; acceptance of the collection by those in Jerusalem will lead those in Jerusalem (rather than "you" as the RSV translation renders it) to glorify God for the spread of the Gospel (13). Further, they will glorify God at "the sincerity of the fellowship with them" (rather than "by the generosity of your contribution for them"); that is, they will glorify God that the Gentiles and the Jews in Jerusalem have been made one in the church of God. Paul then adds that acceptance of the collection will indicate fellowship with all Jews who have accepted Christ. In other words, for Paul the success of the collection will symbolize the unity of Jews and Gentiles in the church. Paul adds that in their prayers those in Jerusalem will express their longing for them as Gentile Christians (14). The basis for the longing would be not so much the personal qualities of the Achaians but the recognition by those in Jerusalem of God's surpassing gift of grace in them. For Paul such recognition would imply admittance of the Gentiles on an equal basis into the church and acceptance of the validity of his gospel free of the law for the Gentiles.

Paul concludes his reflections on the collection with a paean of praise to God for his "inexpressible gift," his son Christ (cf. 8:9). For Paul then the collection is not a tax levied by those in Jerusalem upon the Gentiles. Nor is it simply an act of generosity; nor even is it only an act of love within the body of Christ in which one part provides for the needs of another—although it is this. Rather, more importantly for Paul, the success of the collection manifests God's act in Christ and his reconciliation of Jew and Gentile in the one church through the truth of the gospel.

V. THE LETTER OF TEARS
2 COR 10-13

This section of our present 2 Corinthians seems to be the "Letter of Tears" referred to in 2 Cor 2:3-4. If our historical and literary hypotheses are correct, then this letter was written after Paul's "intermediate" visit to Corinth. Upon his visit to Corinth Paul found his opponents there; he also found among the members of the Corinthian community that some had decided for the opponents. Evidently Paul's visit precipitated a confrontation that resulted in Paul's departure back to Ephesus and his fear of the loss of the Corinthian community to the gospel he preached.

In response to this situation Paul presents in this "Letter of Tears" a stirring and emotional defense of his apostolate and his gospel. It is perhaps these very qualities that have made this section so difficult for interpreters. In addition, this section is difficult to understand because one must distinguish clearly the views of the three parties to the debate: the opponents, the Corinthians, and Paul. Further, in order to understand this section correctly, one must not only reconstruct the views of the opponents but also grasp their charges against Paul. Moreover, it is then necessary to understand the literary genres by which Paul seeks to rebut his opponents and to re-establish his own apostolic authority.

Recent research has provided some very attractive hypotheses concerning these difficult issues. First of all, the opponents of Paul seem to be wandering christian missionaries of jewish origin who boasted of their possession of God's spirit and their consequent ability to perform wonders and to achieve ecstasy. Paul, they charged, showed no signs of such abilities and therefore was a false apostle, a religious charlatan.

In his response, Paul is intent upon unmasking his opponents as the ones who are really false apostles and upon exposing the true nature of his apostolate and his gospel. In order to accomplish this goal, Paul draws upon arguments and styles of argument that were commonplace in his own jewish tradition or in the popular philosophy of his day and that were also appropriate to a letter of apology or defense. In particular, Paul employs the arguments by which the true philosopher was distinguished from the false philosopher or the authentic religious leader from the charlatan. Indeed, in this period the roles of philosopher and religious leader were often combined in the one person and one mission, whether the person were true or false. In his style of argument Paul is willing to use such a popular mode of argument as sarcasm. He is especially adept in using irony; he does not deny directly the charges of his opponents but rather accepts the terms of their charges and then reinterprets or re-evaluates the terms so that what was negative in their eyes becomes positive in the presentation of Paul. In a similar manner Paul uses the literary genre parody, that is, he presents the same type of literary expression as his opponents but reverses the evaluation of it. By such means Paul presents this moving defense of his apostolate and gospel.

The final editor of 2 Corinthians has omitted the opening of the letter with its greeting to the Corinthians, since it was no longer necessary. He has placed this major portion of the "Letter of Tears" at the end of 2 Corinthians in order to serve as a warning that false apostles are expected to appear in the church before the second coming of Christ.

PAUL'S WEAKNESS AND POWER.
2 Cor 10:1-6.

> **10** I, Paul, myself entreat you, by the meekness and gentleness of Christ—I who am humble when face to face with you, but bold to you when I am away!—[2]I beg of you that when I am present I may not have to show boldness with such confidence as I count on showing against some who suspect us of acting in worldly fashion. [3]For though we live in the world we are not carrying on a worldly war, [4]for the weapons of our warfare are not worldly but have divine power to destroy strongholds. [5]We destroy arguments and every proud obstacle to the knowledge of God, and take every thought captive to obey Christ, [6]being ready to punish every disobedience, when your obedience is complete.

Paul probably opened the main body of his "Letter of Tears" with this emphatic beginning "I, Paul, myself." This emphasis serves to indicate the importance of the following exhortations and of Paul's apostolic authority. In his defense against the charges of his opponents, Paul sometimes quotes directly and sometimes reformulates the phrases of his opponents. In vs. 10 Paul quotes their charges to the effect that "his letters are weighty and strong, but his bodily presence is weak, and his speech of no account." For his opponents Paul evidently made too many claims (e.g. to be an apostle of Christ) and demands upon the Corinthians; these claims and demands showed an inappropriate boldness and daring on Paul's part. Further, for them Paul lacked health and strength of body. According to their view, which was a typical view of the age, these faults in Paul's letters and person showed that he was a charlatan rather than a true apostle.

In this response Paul turns here as so often to the example of Christ. He manifested his "meekness and gentleness" by becoming man (cf. Phil 2:6-11) and by suffering upon the cross. Paul then takes the charge of "weakness" (10) and reformulates it as humility. Thus ironically he can then affirm that he is indeed humble when present (1). Thereby, when he is humble, he follows the example of Christ (cf. Phil 2:3) and also manifests to the Corinthians the type of Lord who is presently reigning. Again ironically Paul acknowledges that he is bold when absent, since in him and according to the popular philosophy of the time it was appropriate for the sincere person to be bold for the truth. His exhortation to the Corinthians is that they will so respond that he may continue to imitate Christ by being humble among them. Otherwise, he will have to act boldly and with confidence among them. The basis for his boldness and confidence would be his complete certitude that he has been entrusted with the gospel and called to be an apostle of it (cf. 3:4-7). He will exercise that boldness "against some who suspect us of acting in a worldly fashion." The phrase that is rendered "in a worldly fashion" can be translated more literally "according to the flesh." For Paul the "flesh" can be used in a neutral or in a theological sense. Neutrally it means the person in his/her finitude and mortality. Theologically it means the person as turned away from God and to himself/herself. The charge against Paul is not that he committed particular sinful acts but rather that he was a charlatan, a false religious leader, a false apostle. Paul has reformulated the charge into his own terms of "walking according to the flesh." Those making such accusations were his opponents but also some members of the Corinthian community as vs. 6 makes clear. Paul expands this thought in the same terms by admitting that he is "in the flesh" (or "in the world") in the neutral sense but not acting "according to the flesh" (or "in worldly fashion") in a theological sense. Thereby he also hints at and reacts to the wish of his opponents to be "out of the flesh" by the ascent of the soul and by the experience of religious ecstasy.

It seems clear that Paul's opponents claimed to possess the power of God. In response (4), Paul uses the metaphor of warfare, a metaphor that was often used to speak of the confrontation between true and false religious leader, between wise man and fool (cf. Prov 21:22). He asserts that his weapons are not "fleshly" in the negative theological sense (or "worldly") but "powerful for God." In another context, Paul would identify them as spiritual (cf. 1 Cor 9:11), but here he takes over the term of his opponents in order to use it to his own advantage. His statement that they are "powerful for God" bespeaks his unabashed claim to the Corinthians to be an apostle sent ultimately by God and proximately by Christ. In vss. 4-5 and by means of the military metaphor Paul offers his assessment of his opponents. Their thoughts are against the knowledge of God, although assuredly they have recognized God. Their thoughts are against the obedience of Christ, although they have recognized Christ as one possessed of the divine spirit and able to work wonders. The basis for Paul's assessment lies in his view that true knowledge of God is to be found only in Christ crucified (cf. 5:14-19; 1 Cor 1:18-25). Secondly, it lies in his view that obedience to Christ is faith in him as the crucified and risen Lord of all and not simply as a wonder worker possessed of the spirit.

As an apostle, then, Paul possesses the authority from God and Christ to overcome these false views. Further, he is prepared to punish every disobedience (6), that is, any one of the Corinthian community who falls away from the true gospel proclaimed by Paul. This punishment is to take place when the obedience of the Corinthians is complete. The Corinthians first became obedient to Christ when they accepted the gospel from Paul. Now they have wavered under the influence of the false apostles and begun to accept their false gospel. When the community returns to the true gospel and rejects the false gospel of the opponents, then Paul will be prepared to act against the members of the community who maintain their allegiance to a false gospel.

PAUL'S BOASTING—IN THE LORD.
2 Cor 10:7-18.

[7]Look at what is before your eyes. If any one is confident that he is Christ's, let him remind himself that as he is Christ's, so are we. [8]For even if I boast a little too much of our authority, which the Lord gave for building you up and not for destroying you, I shall not be put to shame. [9]I would not seem to be frightening you with letters. [10]For they say, "His letters are weighty and strong, but his bodily presence is weak, and his speech of no account." [11]Let such people understand that what we say by letter when absent, we do when present. [12]Not that we venture to class or compare ourselves with some of those who commend themselves. But when they measure themselves by one another, and compare themselves with one another, they are without understanding.

[13]But we will not boast beyond limit, but will keep to the limits God has apportioned us, to reach even to you. [14]For we are not overextending ourselves, as though we did not reach you; we were the first to come all the way to you with the gospel of Christ. [15]We do not boast beyond limit, in other men's labors; but our hope is that as your faith increases, our field among you may be greatly enlarged, [16]so that we may preach the gospel in lands beyond you, without boasting of work already done in another's field. [17]"Let him who boasts, boast of the Lord." [18]For it is not the man who commends himself that is accepted, but the man whom the Lord commends.

In this section Paul turns more directly to the claims and charges of his opponents. It seems clear that they assert that they belong to Christ and have authority. Further, this section (12) recalls that the opponents have letters of recommendation (cf. 3:1-4) and reports of their wonder-working activity as part of their recommendation. In addition, Paul alludes to their boasting of their accomplishments. The purpose of such boasting would have been not so much to deprive God of glory but rather to provide evidence that God's power was present within them as religious leaders, as "divine men" (divine in the sense of possessing the divine spirit).

To counter this view Paul casts the dispute in terms of the confrontation between the wise person and the fool in biblical tradition and between the philosopher and sophist, the authentic religious leader and the charlatan in Hellenistic tradition. His argument throughout the section is that self-boasting is the sign of the sophist, the false philosopher, the false apostle. On the other hand, for Paul as for many of his contemporaries boasting is only allowed to defend oneself or to assist others in the service of the truth. Even then such boasting is subject to the conditions that it be in a measured way and that it not be excessive.

The issue then is who is an authentic apostle and who preaches the authentic gospel. The problem is who has the adequate evidence to verify his claim. Paul begins to marshal his arguments by appealing to the Corinthians to open their eyes and look at matters; the evidence is not as onesided as they suppose (7). He refers to the claim of the opponents to belong to Christ, which claim they probably understood as meaning that they possessed the same spirit as Christ and thus were his ministers (cf. 11:23). Paul then adds that such a person as any one of his opponents should consider in evaluating himself that Paul too belongs to Christ. For Paul, however, the sense would be that he is under the reign of the crucified and risen Christ.

Then Paul turns to the issue of authority. In contrast to his opponents' claim to authority and boast of authority, Paul adds that even if he should boast very excessively about his authority, he would not be "put to shame," that is, shown actually to be without authority (8). Paul pointedly adds two qualifications to his authority. First, it is an authority not on his own (as his opponents would claim), but an authority which the Lord has given to him. Second, alluding to the present tension within the community, Paul adds that it is an authority intended by the Lord for the "building up" of the Corinthians rather than for "destroying" them. Paul hints that if necessary, he will be severe with the disobedient members of the Corinthian community, those who reject the true gospel (cf. 13:10); the hint is evidently to the possibility of excommunication. Alluding to the charge that the claims he makes in his letters are too great, Paul ironically states that he will forebear making such a boast of his authority in order that he "might not seem to be frightening them (you) with letters" (9). Thereby, nevertheless, Paul effectively asserts that he does possess apostolic authority.

Then Paul quotes the charge of his opponents, a charge that possibly was vocalized in a confrontation at a meeting among the opponents, the Corinthians, and Paul before Paul's departure from Corinth. The charge is that his letters are "weighty and strong"; they make great claims and assertions about authority and apostolicity. Probably the opponents had in mind at least 1 Corinthians (cf. ch. 9) and the "Letter of Defense" (2 Cor 2:14-6:13; 7:2-4). In contrast to these claims, they charge that his appearance is weak and thus does not provide the evidence to justify the claims according to their criteria—quite the opposite in fact. Again his lack of great rhetorical skill is evidence in their mind that he lacks the spirit and thus lacks the authority which he claims. Paul warns such opponents that the authority which he exercises verbally by letters while absent will be exercised factually by his person when he is present (11).

Paul next turns to the issue of recommendations and their relation to apostolic authority. Paul's opponents have letters of recommendation, which attest their performance of wonders and thus on the basis of this evidence their authority as apostles. In contrast, they charge that since Paul has no such letters, he is recommending himself and thus has no evidence of his apostolic authority beyond his own claim (cf. 3:1-3; 5:12). In response, Paul charges that they in fact are the ones who are recommending themselves. By pointing to their new life and their possession of power, they rather than God are recommending themselves, whether they are aware of this fact or not. Paul ironically states that he would not dare to judge himself as among such persons or to compare himself with such persons (12). He then adds that by looking at only one another and by using only their own criteria of evidence, his opponents lack any proper objective standard by which to measure themselves. Therefore, they have no correct understanding (12). They are akin to the sophist and the charlatan.

Paul then places himself on the side of the true philosopher and the true religious leader when he says that if he should boast, he would do so in a measured way, within "limits." For him the proper measure is the standard (this translation is preferable to "the limits") which God has set before him to preach the gospel to the Gentiles. Thus Paul can assert that he has acted in accord with that standard by coming to the Corinthians (13). Like the true philosopher or religious leader of his age, Paul denies that he is over-extending himself. He is measuring by the proper standard since he did in fact come to the Corinthians and since he was the first one to come to them to preach the gospel of Christ. For Paul, if one were to boast at all, one would have to boast of one's own accomplishments. It would be entirely inappropriate and the sign of sophistry to boast or praise oneself for the accomplishments of someone else. Paul denies that he is boasting of someone else's work, and thereby implicitly accuses his opponents of so doing by entering and claiming as their own the Corinthian community, which was brought to Christ by Paul (15).

Paul complicates and develops further the imagery of measuring and proper size. He has denied that he has exceeded the proper standard of measurement for himself whereas his opponents have. He continues that he does hope to be enlarged ("by God" understood). As the faith of the Corinthians increases, so Paul (or less metaphorically "his field") is enlarged among the Corinthians to such an extent that there is an abundance. This abundance, Paul adds, is not an overextension beyond his proper measure but an abundance in accord with his standard (rather than "limit") of preaching to the Gentiles. Thus, through their increase he is able to preach the gospel in the regions beyond the Corinthians (16), that is, Rome and Spain (cf. Rom 15:22-25). In less figurative language, when the Corinthians cease wavering in the gospel, reject the false gospel of the opponents, and return wholeheartedly to the true gospel, then Paul can be confident of their faith and can continue his mission to other areas of the Gentiles. Thereby, he will not be entering into christian communities already established or praising himself for work already done by someone else and thus by the standard (rather than "field") set for someone else by God.

As the climax to his treatment of the issue of boasting, Paul turns to the biblical tradition. He quotes from Jer 9:22-23 that he who boasts should boast in the Lord (17). Paul then acknowledges a proper boasting. However, it is a boasting not of what a person has done but of what the Lord has done for a person or of what commission the Lord has given to a person. He concludes this portion of his discussion concerning the evidence for an apostle with an ironical principle. His opponents have charged him with commending himself. Paul has argued that they in fact are the ones who commend themselves. The principle that Paul puts forth is that the only person approved or authenticated as an apostle is the one whom the Lord commends rather than the one who commends himself (18). In the ensuing chapters Paul will show that the sign of the Lord's approval is that the true apostle bears the true gospel in his life as well as in his teaching, a life therefore that is modeled on the suffering and death of the Lord.

FOOLISHNESS AND YET TRUTH.
2 Cor 11:1-12:13.

This entire section 2 Cor 11:1-12:13 is placed by Paul under the theme of foolishness. He opens it with a reference to foolishness (11:1) and continually reminds his readers of this theme (cf. 11:16,17,19,21; 12:6,11). He uses this theme of foolishness and the related means of irony and parody because they provide the only way which he can use to expose his opponents before the Corinthians and to assist the Corinthians to see the truth.

In the Hellenistic world the fool was not a jester but a person who had lost the correct measure of himself and the world around him. The true philosopher was often portrayed as a fool, especially by the sophists, because he was judged to have lost the measure. In fact, for the audience the philosopher had replaced the apparent measure of the sophists by the true measure. Thus in his foolishness the true philosopher ultimately and ironically spoke the truth.

Since his opponents had charged Paul with being a false apostle, Paul responds in the style of the philosopher responding to the sophist. He assumes the role of the fool in order to expose the weakness of his opponents' position and to bring the Corinthians to the truth. Paul can presume that the Corinthians, as participants in Hellenistic culture, will not fail to notice the style of his discussion and the force of his arguments.

FALSE APOSTLES AND A FALSE GOSPEL.
2 Cor 11:1-6.

> **11** I wish you would bear with me in a little foolishness. Do bear with me! [2]I feel a divine jealousy for you, for I betrothed you to Christ to present you as a pure bride to her one husband. [3]But I am afraid that as the serpent deceived Eve by his cunning, your thoughts will be led astray from a sincere and pure devotion to Christ. [4]For if some one comes and preaches another Jesus than the one we preached, or if you receive a different spirit from the one you received, or if you accept a different gospel from the one you accepted, you submit to it readily enough. [5]I think that I am not in the least inferior to these superlative apostles. [6]Even if I am unskilled in speaking, I am not in knowledge; in every way we have made this plain to you in all things.

Paul opens this passage and the theme of foolishness by entreating the Corinthians to put up with some foolishness on his part (1). As the later verse (3) indicates, Paul is fearful of the loss of the Corinthian community because of the success of his opponents. His fear is not so much of their loss from him as from the gospel. He is jealous for them; again his concern is not for the protection of his accomplishments but for God's sake (2). To develop his concern for them Paul uses the image of betrothal or engagement (3). According to this image Paul, perhaps in the role of the father of the bride, has betrothed or arranged the engagement of the Corinthians as a chaste virgin to one man, Christ. The betrothal would have occurred when Paul preached the gospel to the Corinthians and they accepted it. The presentation to Christ for the marriage would then occur at the second coming (cf. the marriage of Yahweh and his people in the Old Testament and the marriage feast as the image of God's final Kingdom). The task then of the virgin during the interim period would be to remain steadfastly loyal to the man to whom she was betrothed. For Paul the issue at Corinth is not basically an issue of loyalty to one apostle or another but of loyalty to Christ and thus to the gospel.

Paul then extends the image by an example of disloyalty —Eve (3). He recalls the account in Genesis that the serpent led Eve astray (Gen 3:4,13). In accord with later jewish tradition he also associates the serpent with Satan and possibly hints that the serpent led her astray by seduction. Paul attributes this success of the serpent to his "cunning." Paul then makes quite clear his assessment of the force behind his opponents; it is the serpent, that is, Satan (cf. 11:14). Behind the reference to the "cunning" of the serpent, there is probably the allusion that on the one hand Paul's opponents have accused him of being "cunning" (12:16) and that on the other hand in the traditional argument of the period the true philosopher labels the sophist as "cunning." Paul's fear then is that through these apostles Satan will disturb the whole-hearted allegiance of the Corinthians to Christ.

Paul alludes to these apostles in the generalizing phrase, "If someone comes" (4). They are said to preach "another Jesus," a "different spirit," and a "different gospel." In themselves these phrases are enigmatic, and scholars have disagreed over their implications. A more recent hypothesis, which we have followed in this commentary, suggests that in the context of the whole epistle "another Jesus" for these opponents is simply an earthly, wonder-working Jesus rather than the crucified and risen Lord. "Another spirit" is the spirit of power and ecstasy, which this other Jesus and these false apostles possessed, rather than the Spirit from God and Christ, which brings about the new life of the new aeon in the Christian (cf. Rom 6:1-11). "Another gospel" is the message about the power, which Jesus experienced and demonstrated in his life and which these false apostles now possess, rather than the message about the suffering, crucified Lord.

Paul has asked the Corinthians to put up with him for, as he says with great irony, they receive well such other apostles. He continues then with what seems to be both an ironical and arrogant outburst. He claims that he is in no way "inferior to these superlative apostles" (5). Certainly the use of the term "superlative" for these apostles is ironical. Paul's claim to be equal to them seems at first sight to be somewhat arrogant as indeed the claim of his opponents is. But in the context Paul has placed this remark within his speech as a fool (11:1). Thereby, he recognizes that only a fool would make such a claim; but he also knows that his audience—the Corinthians—will recognize the truth of his claim to be an apostle.

Paul then continues his attack upon these apostles with regard to the subject of speech. Evidently his opponents had boasted of their rhetorical skill and ecstatic speech. Both were signs of their possession of the spirit and evidence for their apostolic commission. Further, they attacked Paul for his lack of rhetorical skill and ecstatic speech and argued to the Corinthians that such a lack demonstrated his lack of the spirit and lack of apostolate. Paul admits the charge that he is a layman in speech ("unskilled in speaking") and turns even that to his advantage. In the clash between philosopher and sophist in the period, the philosopher often claimed to lack rhetorical skill even though he, like Paul, might actually be quite eloquent. The statement was meant to ensure the audience that they were hearing the truth and not merely rhetorical tricks. After acknowledging then his lack of skill in speaking, Paul asserts his familiarity with knowledge (6), that is, the knowledge of the gospel. The Corinthians were concerned about true knowledge that came from the Spirit (cf. 1 Cor 8:1). For Paul that knowledge was to be found in the message about Christ crucified and risen. He is familiar with that knowledge of the gospel since he manifests it both in his preaching and in his life to the Corinthians (6).

SUPPORT FOR AN APOSTLE.
2 Cor 11:7-15.

> [7]Did I commit a sin in abasing myself so that you might be exalted, because I preached God's gospel without cost to you? [8]I robbed other churches by accepting support from them in order to serve you. [9]And when I was with you and was in want, I did not burden any one, for my needs were supplied by the brethren who came from Macedonia. So I refrained and will refrain from burdening you in any way. [10]As the truth of Christ is in me, this boast of mine shall not be silenced in the regions of Achaia. [11]And why? Because I do not love you? God knows I do!
>
> [12]And what I do I will continue to do, in order to undermine the claim of those who would like to claim that in their boasted mission they work on the same terms as we do. [13]For such men are false apostles, deceitful workmen, disguising themselves as apostles of Christ.
>
> [14]And no wonder, for even Satan disguises himself as an angel of light. [15]So it is not strange if his servants also disguise themselves as servants of righteousness. Their end will correspond to their deeds.

As the Corinthians assess the evidence for an apostle, Paul suggests that the next issue to be considered by them is that of support for an apostle. In that period it was debated whether the philosopher and religious leader (or missionary) should receive support or pay for his labors. For some ancients, such as Paul's opponents, acceptance of support was attestation of the authenticity of one's mission. The converse was also true; non-acceptance meant for them non-authenticity of apostolate. For others, acceptance of money for teaching the truth or performing religious activity was the sure sign of sophistry or charlatanery, whereas the true philospher or religious figure presented himself gratuitously. Paul in 1 Cor 9:4-18 vociferously defends the right of an apostle to support. He even accepted support from other churches; yet he never accepted support from the Corinthians. Paul's reason for this particular refusal is not clear. Perhaps he feared that he would be considered simply as another professional sophist and rhetorician in that community. In any case, his refusal to accept support provided his opponents with another argument against Paul's apostolic mission. His refusal, they argued, showed that he was aware that he was not an apostle.

In response, Paul first exaggerates the charge when he asks if he committed a sin in preaching the gospel of God to them freely (7). Further, he casts the issue in his own theological terms. He hints at the humiliation and exaltation of Christ (cf. Phil 2:6-11) and then asks rhetorically if he committed sin in humbling himself, not so that he might be exalted but so that they might be exalted. In this question Paul makes clear his view that the life of an apostle should follow the life of his Lord. He admits that he has accepted support from other churches for the sake of his ministry in Corinth (8) and adds that other Christians from Macedonia assisted him in his need during his ministry in Corinth (9). In an oath formula Paul asserts that he will keep to this practice in the churches of Achaia (10). With the striking

irony of the fool, he states that this, his boast, will not be
silenced. He denies that the motivation behind this practice is lack of love for them (11). Rather, he will maintain
this practice in the future because of the claims and charges
of his opponents (12). Exactly why he will maintain this
practice is not clear in the Greek. The RSV translates "in
order to undermine the claim of those who would like to
claim that in their boasted mission they work on the same
terms as we do," that is, both Paul and his opponents would
preach the gospel and receive pay. An alternate and probably better translation, which maintains the irony and the
theme of the fool's speech, would read "in order to cut off
the opportunity from those who would like an opportunity
(and) in order that in what they boast they may be found even
as we are," namely, fools. Paul's point is first that they seek
an opportunity to place Paul on the same level as themselves
by using their categories of judging evidence for apostolate
and second that boasting of reception or non-reception of
support is foolishness.

Paul clearly states then (13) his assessment of these opponents; they are false apostles and deceitful missionaries
("workers"). He hints at their desire to be transformed by
their share in glory through ecstasy (cf. 3:18) and instead
ironically asserts that although they are false apostles,
they have been transformed or "disguised" as apostles of
Christ. Paul then alludes to the later jewish belief that
Satan had changed himself into an angel of light at the time
of the deception of Eve (14). In an argument from the more
difficult to the less difficult he uses this belief to prove the
possibility that Satan's servants have been changed into
or disguised as servants of righteousness (15), i.e. of the
gospel which announces the new relationship between God
and humanity that has been inaugurated by Christ. Paul
concludes his assessment of these opponents by asserting that their end will be in accord with their works:
condemnation.

PAUL'S BOAST AS A FOOL.
2 Cor 11:16-21.

> [16]I repeat, let no one think me foolish; but even if you do, accept me as a fool, so that I too may boast a little. [17](What I am saying I say not with the Lord's authority but as a fool, in this boastful confidence; [18]since many boast of worldly things, I too will boast.) [19]For you gladly bear with fools, being wise yourselves! [20]For you bear it if a man makes slaves of you, or preys upon you, or takes advantage of you, or puts on airs, or strikes you in the face. [21]To my shame, I must say, we were too weak for that!

In this section Paul continues his attack upon his opponents and his discussion with the Corinthians on the evidence for apostolate by retaining the role of the fool. His aim is ultimately to expose the truth of the situation, that is, the true nature of apostleship and the foolishness of his opponents' position. Their boasting in their commendations from other churches, their impressive speech, their wonders, and their manifestations of the spirit are all to be shown as foolish.

Paul opens by ironically asserting that he does not want anyone to think of him as a fool (16). However, even if he is considered to be a fool, he asks to be accepted. His purpose is to boast a little, but only as a fool since for Paul only as a fool may he boast. In order to give a clear signal to the Corinthians of the role that he is assuming, Paul adds that he is not now speaking according to the command and with the authority of the Lord when he boasts (17). Nevertheless, in his role as a fool he will imitate his opponents by boasting (18), even though he recognizes that their boasting (the "many") is actually in a manner turned away from God. We shall see that his boasting is of a different character.

In a pointedly ironic sentence Paul praises the Corinthians for being wise and offers his assessment of his opponents. The Corinthians have been wise enough and have accepted the true fools (his opponents); now they should at least accept the one who is playing the role of the fool, Paul (19). The type of wisdom shown by the Corinthians is further ironically characterized in figurative language. Paul praises their wisdom in submitting themselves to the rule of these missionaries, in supporting them, in accepting their claim to apostolic authority, in acknowledging their claim to special spiritual status, and in allowing themselves to be considered as of less spiritual value than these missionaries. With a glance at his own apostolic work among the Corinthians, Paul ironically acknowledges to his own disgrace that it seems as if he has been weak (21). It seems so since he has not exercised a similar power to despoil them. The irony consists in the fact that he has indeed been weak in the opponents' sense of performing wonders but that it is this very weakness which manifests the crucified Lord and which presents the power of God in preaching the gospel.

THE ORIGINS OF AN APOSTLE.
2 Cor 11:21-23.

> But whatever any one dares to boast of—I am speaking as a fool—I also dare to boast of that. [22]Are they Hebrews? So am I. Are they Israelites? So am I. Are they descendants of Abraham? So am I. [23]Are they servants of Christ?

As Paul begins his fool's boast, he turns to the issue of the proper origins of one who would be considered as an apostle. It is clear from these verses that Paul's opponents were christian missionaries of jewish origin. They claim to be "Hebrew," jewish in the sense of blood descendants rather than proselytes; perhaps this term also indicates their native language of Hebrew and/or Aramaic. If so, the starting point of these missionaries would probably have been Palestine. Further, they claim to be Israelites, those who share socially and religiously in the jewish heritage. In addition they claim to be "descendants of Abraham," heirs of the promises made by God to Abraham and his descendants (cf. Gal 3:16,19,29). It is striking that these opponents do not claim to be "Jews" as such. It probably was the case that the term "Jew" was associated with anti-Semitism in that period and also that the other terms had the desired, richer connotations of religious and social heritage. For their christian claim these opponents stated that they were "servants of Christ," not simply ministers at table or assistants in charitable distributions but proclaimers of their own gospel message. In response, Paul asserts that he can make equal or better claims. Therefore, the Corinthians should conclude that these claims do not establish the authenticity of an apostle and are ultimately foolish.

For Paul the significance attached to the claims by these opponents was a more important issue than the claims themselves. For the opponents these claims asserted the continuing validity of their religious tradition. According to them the aeon and the dispensation of Abraham, Moses, and the Scriptures were still in force. For Paul the old aeon and old dispensation had passed; the promises had been fulfilled in Christ. Thus in the new aeon the only matter of importance was being "in Christ." To boast of other external matters, which had passed away was really foolishness. Therefore, as Paul acknowledges his foolishness in making these claims, his ironical attack upon the opponents for basing their self-estimation upon these claims becomes obvious.

THE WONDERS OF AN APOSTLE.
2 Cor 11:23-33.

> I am a better one—I am talking like a madman—with far greater labors, far more imprisonments, with countless beatings, and often near death. [24]Five times I have received at the hands of the Jews the forty lashes less one. [25]Three times I have been beaten with rods; once I was stoned. Three times I have been shipwrecked; a night and a day I have been adrift at sea; [26]on frequent journeys,

in danger from rivers, danger from robbers, danger from my own people, danger from Gentiles, danger in the city, danger in the wilderness, danger at sea, danger from false brethren; [27]in toil and hardship, through many a sleepless night, in hunger and thirst, often without food, in cold and exposure. [28]And, apart from other things, there is the daily pressure upon me of my anxiety for all the churches. [29]Who is weak, and I am not weak? Who is made to fall, and I am not indignant?

[30]If I must boast, I will boast of the things that show my weakness. [31]The God and Father of the Lord Jesus, he who is blessed for ever, knows that I do not lie. [32]At Damascus, the governor under King Aretas guarded the city of Damascus in order to seize me, [33]but I was let down in a basket through a window in the wall, and escaped his hands.

In this passage Paul takes up the issue of wonders as a sign of the authenticity of an apostle. It seems clear that his opponents boasted of their accomplishments, their demonstrations of divine power, their wonders (cf. 12:12). In addition, their letters of recommendation probably attested their success and contained lists of their wonders or miracles as proof of their possession of the divine spirit (the technical term for such a list is an "aretalogy"). In response, Paul takes up this issue of wonders but plays the part of the wise fool. As a fool, he too will boast; but foolishly he will boast in his sufferings rather than in his successes. Further, as a wise fool, he will adopt a tactic often employed in the debates between the sages and the sophists of that day. Whereas the sophist presented himself as the successful, talented philosopher, the true philosopher or sage showed and was expected to show that he had endured trials and tribulations for the sake of his convictions and had not wavered from them. Thus the sage preferred a list of his trials as the sign of his authenticity. As the wise fool, then, Paul counters his opponents' list of wonders with his own list, a list of trials, in order to expose the ultimate sophistry of his opponents' claims.

As a wandering missionary there is no doubt that Paul experienced many trials. In the Acts of the Apostles there are several accounts of trials, which Paul is said to have endured. However, even the accounts in the Acts of the Apostles do not record all the trials which Paul lists in this section. Further, in his "Letter of Defense" Paul has already listed his trials (6:4-5). Here his list is more complete. In considering this list it is better to focus attention less upon the typical trials of the sage and more upon the atypical elements in order to discern Paul's real concerns. Finally, Paul presents his list of trials not simply because they have tactical value in dealing with his opponents but more importantly because for him suffering is appropriate to the gospel which he preaches. Any apostle of a Lord who suffered on the cross and is now risen must also suffer; indeed, his sufferings "in Christ" manifest the presence of and the type of Lord whom he serves.

After listing his afflictions in general (23), Paul presents the punishments he has endured (24)—the jewish scourging which is forty stripes minus one (cf. Deut 25:3), the Roman flogging (25; cf. Acts 16:22-24), and stoning (cf. Acts 14:19). In addition, he mentions his involvement in shipwrecks (cf. Acts 27:14-44). Then he lists the continual and daily threats to the wandering missionary (26). Notable among the threats are the dangers from his own race (cf. Acts 9:23,29) and the dangers from the Gentiles (cf. Acts 16:20). The distinctive element in these threats, however, is the danger from "false brethren." With this term Paul hints at the past troubles he has encountered in his mission (cf. Gal 2:4) and the present split within the community. After a list of physical difficulties (27) Paul then reaches the climax of all his trials, "the daily pressure upon me of my anxiety for all the churches" (28). As a founder of various communities, Paul's continual concern and care for them is that of love. For Paul the truest sign of an apostle is not one's performance of wonders but rather one's love for the community. Paul then expands this thought with reference to the present situation in Corinth (29). He is weak along with those in Corinth who are weak in the sense that they are without power to perform wonders. He is angered when the Corinthians are led astray from the true gospel and the work of the Lord is threatened with destruction. As a summary of the varying positions, Paul picks up the slogan of his opponents that "it is necessary to boast" and adds that if this is the case, then he will boast not in his wonders but in his weakness.

In vss. 31-32 Paul suddenly switches the topic to his escape from Damascus. The shift in topic is so sudden that some commentators consider these verses to be a later addition. However, it seems more likely that these verses are original and that they continue the theme of weakness. In contrast with a wondrous escape that would manifest the presence of divine power (cf. the Exodus), Paul tells the humorous story of his escape in a basket. His solemn oath that he is not lying emphasizes even more the humor of the story and points out the presence of God in this weakness rather than in some wonder.

BOASTING IN VISIONS AND REVELATION.
2 Cor 12:1-12.

> **12** I must boast; there is nothing to be gained by it, but I will go on to visions and revelations of the Lord. ²I know a man in Christ who fourteen years ago was caught up to the third heaven—whether in the body or out of the body I do not know, God knows. ³And I know that this man was caught up into Paradise—whether in the body or out of the body I do not know, God knows—⁴and he heard things that cannot be told, which man may not utter. ⁵On behalf of this man I will boast, but on my own behalf I will not boast, except of my weaknesses. ⁶Though if I wish to boast, I shall not be a fool, for I shall be speaking the truth. But I refrain from it, so that no one may think more of me than he sees in me or hears from me.

[7]And to keep me from being too elated by the abundance of revelations, a thorn was given me in the flesh, a messenger of Satan, to harass me, to keep me from being too elated. [8]Three times I besought the Lord about this, that it should leave me; [9]but he said to me, "My grace is sufficient for you, for my power is made perfect in weakness." I will all the more gladly boast of my weaknesses, that the power of Christ may rest upon me.

[10]For the sake of Christ, then, I am content with weaknesses, insults, hardships, persecutions, and calamities; for when I am weak, then I am strong.

[11]I have been a fool! You forced me to it, for I ought to have been commended by you. For I am not at all inferior to these superlative apostles, even though I am nothing. [12]The signs of a true apostle were performed among you in all patience, with signs and wonders and mighty works.

This passage is the final section of Paul's boast as a fool. In this passage the topic is that of visions and revelations. Paul's opponents had boasted of their mystical experiences in order to demonstrate their authenticity as apostles. Paul's purpose in this section, on the other hand, is to show that such boasting is foolish and does not accomplish its goal. To attain this purpose Paul uses parody; he mocks the accounts of his opponents in order to show their lack of value as proof. He then offers what he considers the only true criterion of an apostle, service to the community.

In that period there were numerous accounts of the ascent of the person to heaven where he saw and heard the secrets of heaven which were not to be communicated by the seer to all human beings but only to those chosen by God. Especially in Hellenistic circles or in Hellenized Judaism it was considered that the soul separated from the body and ascended to heaven. Evidently such visions were expected by the Corinthians as a part of religious life and were claimed by the opponents as proof of their apostolate.

Paul begins his parody of his opponents' claims by employing their slogan "it is necessary to boast" (1). Paul agrees with the slogan but undercuts its value and hints at the genre of his language by adding that "there is nothing to be gained by it." For Paul the question of gain is the question of contribution to building up the church (cf. 8:10; cf. 1 Cor 6:12). In accord with the view of his age that the wise person does not boast of himself (only the sophist does), Paul distinguishes between himself and "a man in Christ" as he recounts this ascent (2). In contrast to his opponents who probably recounted frequent and recent ascents to heaven, Paul refers to an event some fourteen years previously. In mockery of his opponents' certitude that the soul ascends to heaven, Paul states that he does not know whether the soul or the person ascended and leaves such knowledge to God. In accord with a customary conception of that era, there were considered to be three heavens: the heaven of the planets, the heaven of the fixed stars, and the final heaven in which God resided. In vs. 3 Paul repeats these ideas but varies them slightly. According to this verse the man was snatched up to Paradise, a part of the third heaven in which the blessed were thought to dwell after their death or after the final judgment (4). Further, he adds that this man heard the divine secrets, which were customarily to be communicated to God's elect, but then he states that these secrets cannot be told. Like his opponents he claims a vision; unlike his opponents he does not report the divine secrets heard and thus does not provide a proof of the actuality of the vision. Thereby, Paul hopes to convince his Corinthians that the claim to visions by his opponents proves nothing. Paul continues in his role as a fool in that he will boast about such a man who had this vision (5). As the wise fool he makes the only proper boast about himself when he boasts paradoxically in his weakness.

Briefly Paul drops the mask of the fool in vss. 6-7. Like the true philosopher who confronts the boasting sophist,

Paul asserts that if he wanted to boast, he would not speak foolishness but rather state the truth. Further, he adds that he will spare the Corinthians even this truth so that they will judge him only on what they see and hear from him. His weakness of presence and lack of impressive speech (cf. 10:10) are real and thus prevent him from being evaluated as an apostle by the false criteria of presence and speech; for Paul the only criterion will be service of the community.

Paul then returns to the role of a fool and his parody of his opponents on the subject of revelations. Revelations are evaluated by his opponents as one of the signs of a true apostle. Further, for his opponents the true apostle should be healthy as a sign of his possession of the divine spirit and should be able to heal by that same spirit. In his foolishness Paul claims an abundance of revelations (7). He hints at his assessment of his opponents in their claims by adding that something was given to him in order that he might not be "elated" or puffed up. Contrary to what was expected of a true apostle by his opponents, Paul states that he was given "a thorn in the flesh." Probably this enigmatic phrase refers to some physical illness, which is considered to be a result of demonic influence. In accord with the proper mode of the era, Paul prays for relief (8) and receives an oracular response from the Lord. Instead of the expected proclamation of cure, however, Paul hears that the Lord's "grace is sufficient for him" and that the Lord's "power is made perfect in weakness." Like his opponents Paul claims a revelation; unlike his opponents he does not report a healing and thus provide a proof of the validity of his apostolate. Again Paul's point to his Corinthians is that the claim to revelations proves nothing. Further, as the fool he boasts in revelations which have no sign of healing; as the wise fool, he speaks the ultimate truth that God's power is revealed in human weakness, that of Christ first and that of the apostle next. Just as the divine presence rested upon Israel of old, so too the power of Christ rests upon the apostle now (9).

As so often throughout this correspondence, Paul then offers a catalogue of trials which he endures for the sake of

Christ (10; cf. 4:10; 6:4-5; 11:23-27). In contrast to his opponents Paul can assert paradoxically that it is precisely when he endures these sufferings for the sake of the gospel that he manifests the presence of Christ as Lord and the power with which Christ reigns as the crucified and risen one.

As a final acknolwedgement of the role that he has been playing, Paul admits that he has been a fool(11). Ironically he adds that he should be commended by the Corinthians since he has lacked nothing in comparison with the superlative apostles. Then he notes that he is nothing. The wise fool admits that he is nothing when he faces the sophist. Paul draws out the "reduction to the absurd" when he equates himself, as nothing, with his opponents. They too are nothing, and their boasting is the true foolishness. Their claim to have performed signs, wonders, and powers as the mark of a true apostle is made equally by Paul (12). But Paul's evidence of his apostolate is the endurance of sufferings for his churches.

AN APOSTLE'S SUPPORT.
2 Cor 12:13-15.

> [13]For in what were you less favored than the rest of the churches, except that I myself did not burden you? Forgive me this wrong!
> [14]Here for the third time I am ready to come to you. And I will not be a burden, for I seek not what is yours but you; for children ought not to lay up for their parents, but parents for their children. [15]I will most gladly spend and be spent for your souls. If I love you the more, am I to be loved the less?

In these verses Paul returns to the issue of support of an apostle (cf. 11:7-12) and further exercises his rhetorical skills. He asks ironically if the Corinthians were less favored except that he did not take money from them (13). He then asks sarcastically to be forgiven this offense. Further, Paul expresses his resolve not to accept support from the

Corinthians in the future (14). As we mentioned earlier (cf. 11:7-12), Paul does not explain why he originally refused to accept support from the Corinthians. It seems likely that he refused support both in the past and for the future because of a fear that the Corinthians could too easily consider him simply as a wandering, paid missionary rather than as an apostle of Christ. As the basis for his refusal Paul suggests that he seeks the Corinthians rather than their possessions. He then quotes what appears to be a proverb to illuminate his position. Parents provide for their children rather than children for their parents. As their spiritual parent (cf. 1 Cor 4:14-15) he is willing to provide for them. Even more Paul is willing not only to provide for them but to spend his very life in the service of the salvation of the Corinthian community (cf. Phil 2:17). In a climax of irony Paul then asks the community if he is to be loved the less by them because of his abundant love for them.

THE COLLECTION:
SUPPORT OR OFFERING.
2 Cor 12:16-18.

> [16]But granting that I myself did not burden you, I was crafty, you say, and got the better of you by guile. [17]Did I take advantage of you through any of those whom I sent to you? [18]I urged Titus to go, and sent the brother with him. Did Titus take advantage of you? Did we not act in the same spirit? Did we not take the same steps?

Now that Paul has answered the charge that he refused support because of his lack of apostolate, he turns to a related but more serious charge. Evidently his opponents had claimed that Paul's collection was merely a clever subterfuge for obtaining support (16). The money to be collected was for himself rather than for the saints in Jerusalem. In response Paul asks the Corinthians if they have in fact been defrauded by those whom he sent (17). Paul had sent Titus and another brother to Corinth prior to his second

("intermediate") visit in order to arrange the collection
(cf. 8:6). The collection, however, had not as yet been taken
up, and thus the charge is without foundation (18). Probably
Paul mentioned here originally the name of the other
brother. If so, it would have been removed by the final
editor in order to give the letter a more general relevance.

VISIT TO A DIVIDED COMMUNITY.
2 Cor 12:19-21.

> [19]Have you been thinking all along that we have been
> defending ourselves before you? It is in the sight of God
> that we have been speaking in Christ, and all for your up-
> building, beloved. [20]For I fear that perhaps I may come
> and find you not what I wish, and that you may find me
> not what you wish; that perhaps there may be quarreling,
> jealousy, anger, selfishness, slander, gossip, conceit, and
> disorder. [21]I fear that when I come again my God may
> humble me before you, and I may have to mourn over
> many of those who sinned before and have not repented
> of the impurity, immorality, and licentiousness which
> they have practiced.

After considering the last charge against him, Paul
reflects upon these last chapters (10-12) and then turns to
his forthcoming visit. As we have mentioned, in the Hellenistic era the sophist or religious charlatan defended himself
by bombast and rhetorical tricks whereas the philosopher
and religious leader defended the truth in simplicity. Paul
aligns himself with the philosopher and religious leader
when he asks the Corinthians (19) if they think he has been
defending himself in these chapters. Rather, he asserts that
he has been speaking as a Christian in the presence of God,
therefore speaking the truth. Further, Paul adds that his
intention is not to defend himself but rather to serve the
community. Again he uses the image of "building up" the
community (cf. 10:8; 13:10).

Concerning his forthcoming visit Paul expresses his fear that he will find the Corinthians not as he wishes (20). It seems clear that Paul's fear is that the Corinthians will not be standing fast in the gospel, that they will have adopted the false gospel of his opponents with its "divine-man" Christology, and that the Corinthians will be more interested in displaying their spiritual powers than showing concern for one another. A related fear by Paul is that the Corinthians may not find him as they wish. Their hope for Paul's appearance with miracles and signs of spiritual accomplishment may be contradicted by the reality of his appearance with apostolic authority and severity (cf. 13:2).

Paul continues his statement of fear by listing the sins that he fears he might find among the Corinthians. For this list Paul uses a catalogue of vices. Such catalogues were frequently used in the Hellenistic period and were often very general in nature. In this case Paul has used the form of the catalogue but selected vices that were specifically appropriate to the situation. The quarreling, jealousy, anger, etc., to which Paul alludes, reflect the situation of a rival mission, a divided community, and a religious view that stresses display of spiritual powers rather than mutual love within the community.

In the following verse (21) Paul continues his statement of fear and mentions other vices but interrupts the catalogue. This formal break in pattern is a signal that Paul is turning his attention to another concern. His fear is that when he comes again God will humble him in the sense that God will show him the failure of the Corinthians to remain in the christian way of life, which he has preached to them. His further fear is that he will have to act forcefully against such disobedience. It seems probable that the reference to a previous sinfulness in impurity, immorality and licentiousness and to lack of repentance is a reference to some still unresolved issues from the period of 1 Corinthians (cf. 1 Cor 5:1-13; 6:12-20). Evidently Paul's second ("intermediate") visit had shown him that the issues were not resolved and that some Corinthians continued in their immoral practices.

A VISIT WITH APOSTOLIC AUTHORITY.
2 Cor 13:1-10.

13 This is the third time I am coming to you. Any charge must be sustained by the evidence of two or three witnesses. [2]I warned those who sinned before and all the others, and I warn them now while absent, as I did when present on my second visit, that if I come again I will not spare them—[3]since you desire proof that Christ is speaking in me. He is not weak in dealing with you, but is powerful in you. [4]For he was crucified in weakness, but lives by the power of God. For we are weak in him, but in dealing with you we shall live with him by the power of God.

[5]Examine yourselves, to see whether you are holding to your faith. Test yourselves. Do you not realize that Jesus Christ is in you?—unless indeed you fail to meet the test! [6]I hope you will find out that we have not failed. [7]But we pray God that you may not do wrong—not that we may appear to have met the test, but that you may do what is right, though we may seem to have failed. [8]For we cannot do anything against the truth, but only for the truth. [9]For we are glad when we are weak and you are strong. What we pray for is your improvement. [10]I write this while I am away from you, in order that when I come I may not have to be severe in my use of the authority which the Lord has given me for building up and not for tearing down.

In this last section Paul repeats that he is coming (1) for the third time (cf. 12:14). His first visit had been the founding visit. His second visit had ended in confrontation with the community and Paul's departure (cf. 2:1-13). This final visit is to decide the issue of the relation between Paul and his community.

Paul views his forthcoming visit in a judicial light. He quotes Deut 19:15, which states that a charge in court must be sustained by two or three witnesses rather than simply by one. Later jewish and christian (cf. Mt 18:16) tradition

extended this rule in that two or three warnings were first to
be given. Paul applies this rule in the sense that his two
visits and his present letter constitute three warnings (2).
Now he is ready to act. He is ready to act against the two
groups that he had mentioned in ch. 12: those who were
sinners (12:21) and all those who had accepted the false
gospel and were guilty of factionalism, envy, anger, etc.
(12:19-20).

His warning is that if he comes, he will not spare them (3).
Evidently his warning is that he will excommunicate and
hand over to Satan (cf. 1 Cor 5:5) those who are unrepentant
sinners and those who have forsaken the true gospel. In 1
Cor 5:1-10 Paul had exercised such authority with the community against an individual offender. Here Paul fears the
loss of the entire community or the majority of the community and warns that he will excommunicate both those
who have accepted another Jesus and unrepentant sinners.

Paul then turns to his motive in exercising such authority
(3). At the instigation of the intruding missionaries the
Corinthians had re-examined Paul's claim to be an apostle
of Christ. Paul had accepted the validity of their questioning
but rejected their criteria for deciding the issue. According
to the opponents and according to the Corinthians in
dependence upon them, Christ should be only powerful
among them; so too Paul as his apostle should be only
powerful among them. Paul would want to assert that Christ
was also weak in his crucifixion and that his apostle too is
weak in the service of his community. Here, however, he
agrees that the risen Christ is now powerful among them.
Thus, the use of his apostolic authority in the act of excommunication will manifest that the risen Christ speaks
through him.

But Paul then hastens to add that the risen Christ is also
Christ crucified (4). He was crucified because of weakness,
not in the sense that he could not avoid death but in the
sense that it was one aspect of God's plan for his son (cf. 8:9).
Similarly Christ lives because of the power of God, not
simply in the sense that God's power raised him but in the

sense that he now exercises God's power in the world. Paul's point is that the apostle must pattern his life after Christ. A more precise translation of Paul's thought here would be as follows: "For we are weak in him, but we shall live with him because of the power of God—and that in relation to you." Paul too is weak in this life as a Christian; he will live with Christ after the parousia because of the same power of God that raised Christ. Paul adds the phrase "and that in relation to you" to refer to the same power of God which Christ exercises after the resurrection and which he manifests paradoxically in the weakness of his apostle but also in his apostle's preaching of the gospel and exercise of apostolic authority.

After his warning to the Corinthians Paul exhorts them to examine themselves. They had tested Paul and the opponents to see who satisfied their requirements for an apostle. But Paul adds that the final test of his apostolate is in the Corinthians themselves. He encourages them to see whether they still accept the true gospel which he preached (5). He asks whether they recognize that Jesus Christ is in them. For Paul "holding to the faith" and "Jesus Christ in you" are synonymous terms. Faith then for him involves the reality of the presence of Christ. If the Corinthians examine themselves, hopefully they will recognize the presence of Christ among them and therefore the legitimacy of Paul's apostolate. If they fail to find the presence of Christ among them, then they must have surrendered the gospel and renounced true christian existence. On this basis Paul expresses his hope that the Corinthians, after first seeing the reality of their own christian existence, will recognize the validity of his life as a Christian and as an apostle.

Paul also makes clear again (cf. 12:19) that his motive is not self-defense. His concern is simply for the community. Moreover, rather than being vindictive with the Corinthians for their betrayal of the gospel and himself, Paul prays that they may remain in the correct form of faith and life (7). He is even willing to appear as if he were wrong and rejected as long as the Corinthians continue to accept the true gospel. As a further explanation of this last thought Paul adds that he "cannot do anything against the truth," that is, the truth of the gospel (8). Although he wishes to be accepted by the Corinthians, he can only do so on the basis of speaking the truth of the gospel.

Without rancor at the Corinthians' betrayal Paul also adds that he rejoices when he is weak—weak in the sense of suffering in the service of the gospel and the community —and when they are strong—strong in their faith (9). In contrast with the Corinthians' desire for a power or strength which is expressed in spiritual displays, for Paul true strength is expressed by fidelity to the gospel. He then prays that the Corinthians may be set right with respect to the gospel and to one another. Further, he adds that the purpose of his letter is thier restoration. He hopes to avoid the need to be severe and to exclude the community from those who are in Christ (10). The authority he has as an apostle is to preach the gospel and to establish a community based on the gospel and on mutual love of one another. This goal is the Lord's intention and Paul's desire. However, that authority also involves the right to exclude when necessary (cf. 10:8), a right that Paul hopes to avoid exercising.

CONCLUSION:
EXHORTATIONS, GREETINGS AND BLESSING.
2 Cor 13:11-14.

> [11]Finally, brethren, farewell. Mend your ways, heed my appeal, agree with one another, live in peace, and the God of love and peace will be with you. [12]Greet one another with a holy kiss. [13]All the saints greet you.
> [14]The grace of the Lord Jesus Christ and the love of God and the fellowship of the Holy Spirit be with you all.

During the period in which Paul wrote, letters were often concluded by greetings, a wish for health and a farewell. Paul modifies this pattern slightly in his letters since he concludes them with greetings and then with a blessing, which serves the purpose of the wish for health and the farewell. In this particular letter Paul expands his conclusion by offering his final exhortations before he adds his greetings and blessing.

After a word of farewell Paul enters into his final exhortations, which sum up his concerns in the preceding chapters and the needs of the community (11). He exhorts the Corinthians to set themselves aright (the cognate term is used in vs. 7). He appeals to them to return to the gospel, to end their factionalism, and to restore peace within the community. He assures them that if they reestablish themselves as a community of mutual love which is based upon the gospel, God will be present among them with his love and peace.

Paul next invites the Corinthians to "greet one another with a holy kiss" (12). Evidently the kiss was a part of the community gathering of the Pauline church (cf. Rom 16:16; 1 Cor 16:20; 1 Thess 5:26). It probably followed the prayers and readings of the gathering and preceded the benediction, which opened the Supper. Presupposing that his letter would be read publicly to the community gathering, Paul then asks the members to greet one another as he would if he were present. Further, he sends the greetings of his fellow-Christians, presumably those of Ephesus from which he is writing, to the Corinthians.

The final benediction of this letter is more detailed than usual for Paul. Normally he refers only to the Lord (cf. Rom 16:20; 1 Cor 16:23). In this case, he refers to the Lord and then also to God and the Spirit (cf. 1 Cor 12:4-6; Phil 2:1). Even this final blessing seems to be pertinent to the situation at Corinth since Paul prays for the Corinthians' maintenance in the christian life. He prays that the gift manifested in Christ Jesus and the love exercised in Christ's death and present reign and the fellowship of Christians with Christ and with one another created by the Spirit may be with the Corinthians. In other words, he prays that they may remain faithful to the gospel which they have received and that they may experience it more deeply.

FOR FURTHER READING

1. General Reading

E.B. Allo, *Saint Paul: Seconde Epître aux Corinthiens.* Etudes bibliques. (2nd ed.; Paris: Gabalda, 1956).

   A major, scientific commentary representative of French Catholic scholarship.

C.K. Barrett, *The Second Epistle to the Corinthians.* Harper's New Testament Commentaries. (New York & London: Harper and Row, 1973).

   A very readable and scholarly commentary on 2 Corinthians. Barrett reports on recent scholarship and analyzes the arguments. He himself adopts the view that chaps. 1-9 were the original letter and that chaps. 10-13 were the major part of another letter written after chaps. 1-9.

G. Bornkamm, "The History of the Origin of the So-Called Second Letter to the Corinthians," *The Authorship and Integrity of the New Testament.* Theological Collections 4. (London: Society for the Promotion of Christian Knowledge, 1965) 73-91.

   A brief but important essay which first presented the hypothesis that 2 Corinthians was a compilation of five letters from Paul to the Corinthians.

R. Dillon, "The Second Letter to the Corinthians," *The Jerome Biblical Commentary.* (Ed. R. Brown, S.S.; J. Fitzmyer, S.J.; R. Murphy, O. Carm; Englewood Cliffs: Prentice-Hall, 1968) 276-90.

   A brief but readable commentary, which maintains the traditional view of the unity of 2 Corinthians.

J. Héring, *The Second Epistle of Saint Paul to the Corinthians.* Commentaire du Nouveau Testament. (London: Epworth, 1967).

   A brief but often stimulating commentary.

2. More Specialized Works

C.K. Barrett, *The Signs of An Apostle*. (Philadelphia: Fortress, 1972).

A readable discussion of what apostles were in the New Testament and of what the marks of apostolicity should be for the church.

G. Bornkamm, *Paul*. (New York: Harper and Row, 1969).

A presentation of the results of current, critical German scholarship on the life and thought of Paul. It is designed for the general reader.

J.-F. Collange. *Enigmes de la deuxième Epître de Paul aux Corinthiens: Etude éxégetique de 2 Cor 2:14-7:4.* Society for New Testament Studies, Monograph Series 18. (Cambridge: Cambridge University, 1972).

An extensive study of 2 Cor 2:14-7:4, which considers this section as the opening letter in the correspondence between Paul and Corinth that is now collected as 2 Corinthians. He applies the hypothesis of Georgi concerning a "divine man" theology to these chapters.

J. Fitzmyer, S.J., *Pauline Theology: A Brief Sketch*. (Englewood Cliffs: Prentice-Hall, 1967).

A very readable exposition of the main lines of Paul's thought by an eminent American Catholic scholar.

D. Georgi, *The Opponents of Paul in 2 Corinthians*. (Philadelphia: Fortress, 1980).

This important study followed the literary hypothesis of Bornkamm and then studied the religious and cultural tradition upon which the opponents of Paul drew. He relates their tradition to the theme of the "divine man" in the Hellenistic and Hellenistic-Jewish world and then applies this hypothesis especially to chaps. 10-13.